REALISM, REALITY, AND THE FICTIONAL THEORY OF ALAIN ROBBE-GRILLET AND ANAIS NIN

Patricia A. Deduck
Southwest Texas State University

UNIVERSITY
PRESS OF
AMERICA

Hum
PQ
671
D37
1982

Copyright © 1982 by

University Press of America, Inc.
P.O. Box 19101, Washington, D.C. 20036

Library of Congress Cataloging in Publication Data

Deduck, Patricia A.
    Realism, reality, and the functional theory of
Alain Robbe-Grillet and Anais Nin.

    Bibliography: p.
    1. French fiction--20th century--History and
criticism. 2. Robbe-Grillet, Alain, 1922-
--Criticism and interpretation. 3. Nin, Anaïs,
1903-1977--Criticism and interpretation.
I. Title.
PQ671.D37 1982   843'.914'09   82-13549
ISBN 0-8191-2719-1
ISBN 0-8191-2720-5 (pbk.)

To John

TABLE OF
CONTENTS

Preface

This book is a comparative analysis of the fictional theory of Alain Robbe-Grillet and Anaïs Nin. It is designed to acquaint the reader not only with the two writers' theoretical works and ideas, but also with the relation of their theories to the Western mimetic tradition.

The idea, research, and writing of this book covered a period of several years, during which many friends and colleagues contributed their support and encouragement. Among those whom I wish to acknowledge for their help are Claudia Laird, who assisted in the proofreading of the manuscript, and Irma Vasquez, who helped with its typing.

I wish to acknowledge Georges Borchardt, Inc., 136 East 57th Street, New York, New York for permission to quote from Alain Robbe-Grillet's *Pour un Nouveau Roman* (1967), and the Macmillan Company, 866 Third Avenue, New York, New York, for permission to quote from Anaïs Nin's *The Novel of the Future* (1968). The full acknowledgment appears on the page where the first quotation from *The Novel of the Future* begins.

CHAPTER 1

AN ENQUIRY INTO THE MIMETIC ELEMENTS IN THE NOVEL

I

The novel in the twentieth century has been conspicuous in its questioning of traditional modes of perceiving and rendering reality as well as in its attempts to develop methods for representing a reality which more closely reflects the contemporary person's consciousness of self and the world in which he or she lives. Although all art has traditionally adapted itself to changing conceptions of reality, innovative approaches to the novel, in the past, have represented attempts to redefine aims and techniques only within the tradition of Western art and thought. What is truly radical in contemporary novel theory and practice is not the attempt to render reality in new ways and with new techniques, but the attempt to break completely with the traditions of Western art and with the basic philosophical views of that tradition. As Georges Mathieu has pointed out, certain aspects of lyrical non-configuration in painting and in the arts in general point to a new phenomenon which he believes "calls into question the very foundation of 40,000 years of aesthetic activity."[1] Mathieu is not alone in his recognition of the radical implications of modern art; many contemporary intellectual historians, philosophers, and artists have pointed to the philosophical fissures separating the nineteenth and twentieth from preceding centuries — fissures which have found their eventual expression in the arts.

Eugen Weber, for example, in his analysis of the various artistic and intellectual "movements" in Western art (Romanticism, Realism, Naturalism, Symbolism, and Expressionism) declines to treat them as distinctly unique movements, but rather, conceptualizes them as evolutionary facets of one basic impulse: a search for reality and a means to express it after the breakdown of concepts of universal law and truth in the eighteenth century. The underlying distinction between past and twentieth-century quests for reality, he points out, lies in the fact that discoveries of modern science have compelled man to seek a more specified and subjective concept of reality. As this quest continues in the face of such discoveries, hope of realizing the goal of the quest has gradually diminished. Although man might have initially thought the real task of the quest was to discover a reality external to himself, he now, Weber says, "ends by concluding that reality and its laws must be of his own making, that they lie . . . in his own subjective choice."[2] Weber sees the artistic expression of this new attitude manifested in the gradual movement away from the representation of visible reality in the twentieth century and toward the almost exclusive pursuit of the unconscious, the psychological, the dream. The artist's domain, he claims, is "no longer a *corrida*, or even a laboratory or dissecting room: it has become a seance where he, as medium and visionary, pursues his disintegrator's task which is simply to reflect the disintegration going on around us."[3] Weber's analysis of artistic impulse seems somewhat insular, since he focuses so frequently on its negative aspects — the dissolution evident in the breakdown of traditional forms and techniques, and the conscious rejection of traditional artistic goals. He seems to ignore the fact that much modern artistic endeavor represents a conscious attempt to construct as well as to destroy, and also that the novel remains, even in

2

the 1980's, a "laboratory" or "dissecting room" for many artists.

Leonard Meyer, in *Music, the Arts and Ideas*, presents a more thorough analysis of the implications of contemporary art by concentrating on the positive aspects of the developing aesthetic without ignoring its destructive aspects. He describes the new attitude embodied in contemporary art with the phrase "radical empiricism," defining it in its most literal sense as a defiant and emphatic assertion that "the Renaissance is over." In light of the discoveries of modern science, he points out, artists have begun to deny the reality of relationships between man and the universe, as well as the existence of a recognizable and predictable order in nature, and to assert instead a belief in the reality of individual perception. The rejection of universal order, he feels, implies an even more basic rejection: that of the reality of cause and effect. He points out that what the aesthetic of radical empiricism really denies is not the "theoretical possibility of a principle of causation, but the theoretical possibility of isolating any particular event as being the cause of another particular event." As a result, "the world is seen as a single interrelated field or continuum in which everything interacts with — is the 'cause' of — everything else." Therefore, contemporary artists have taken a basically anti-metaphysical stance and have, rather, asserted the plurality of truth and reality. Pluralism manifests itself in the denial of a single set of absolute truths or laws as well as in the positing of a belief that objects do not have an existence independent of the perception of them. Such an attitude, therefore, implies a conception of reality as a potential, continually formed and re-formed by the human mind.

It is interesting that both Weber and Meyer see the nature of reality as the notion around which the crisis in twentieth-century culture and art is focused, and that both point to the discoveries of modern science as the basis for the development of a new cultural orientation to reality and for the complementary development of a new aesthetic. Both point out that as the artist has abandoned traditional conceptions of reality, so too has he abandoned traditional forms and turned to those associated most often with the sciences: abstractions, geometric shapes, concrete data, facts. George Steiner, in his analysis of the dissolution of culture in the twentieth

3

century, has expressed perhaps most succinctly the impact of science on art and the reasons for the intimate dynamic which seems to operate between the two. He feels that the general attitude today is one which itself represents a major break with the culture of the past, and refers to this attitude as "stoic realism." What characterizes this new attitude is that value is placed on the immediate, the present, without nostalgia for the past or hope for the future. He attributes this cultural attitude to the momentous discoveries of science, with the accompanying advances of technology, and concludes that "the disease of enlightened man is his acceptance, itself wholly superstitious, of the superiority of facts to ideas."[5] In examining the impulses of current radical and anti-art, he finds that such endeavors have begun to aspire to goals similar to those of the sciences, engendering what he terms "a poetry of facts." He writes:

> That 'poetry of facts' and realization of the miraculous delicacies of perception in contemporary science already informs literature at those nervepoints where it is both disciplined and under the stress of the future. It is no accident that Musil was trained as an engineer, that Ernst Junger and Nabokov should be serious entomologists, that Broch and Canetti are writers schooled in the exact and mathematical sciences. The special, deepening presence of Valery in one's feelings about the afterlife of culture is inseparable from his own alertness to the alternative poetics, to the 'other metaphysics' of mathematical and scientific pursuit. The instigations of Queneau and of Borges, which are among the most bracing of modern letters, have algebra and astronomy at their back.[6]

Science, since the late nineteenth century, has initiated radical questioning of our conception of the nature of the universe and its physical laws, and in so doing, has transformed our understanding of the concept of reality. The ideals of stability seem no longer

4

tenable; twentieth-century culture embraces phenomena and reality itself in a state of disruption.

It is not surprising, therefore, given the skeptical temper of the sciences and the arts in our century, to find the novel form, previously an outgrowth of a shared notion of the world and reality, undergoing radical transformation. It seems logical to assume that in the arts, as in other areas of human culture, conceptual changes are the basis for and necessitate formal changes of expression. Modern innovations in the arts are the result of a new philosophical orientation to phenomena which demands a new medium for its expression. As Michel Butor notes, ". . . toute véritable transformation de la forme romanesque, toute féconde recherche dans ce domaine, ne peut que se situer à l'intérieur d'une transformation de la notion même de roman."[7]

The theory of art which had prevailed from classical times affirmed above all an intimate relation between art and reality; that is, that art was *mimesis*, an "imitation" or "representation" of life. The mimetic theory did not simply imply a copying of life, of the sort produced by photographic exactitude; rather, as Aristotle proposed, art was imitative insofar as it was creative, insofar as it was constructed by the interpreting, shaping consciousness of the poet. Art did not reflect life as a mirror did, but reflected the very process of life: a becoming.[8] Reality, however, was recognized as residing in the objective, external world, and art was an imitation of this objective form. The idea that imitation of nature — the reproduction of natural objects and actions — is a realistic portrayal of life, held precedence for centuries.

John Boyd, in his study of the mimetic tradition, describes mimesis as reflective of an objective impulse and places the beginning of its decline at the end of the eighteenth century. It was at this point that the concept, although not in any sense totally rejected, was replaced by an emphasis on the subjective impulses of art. This development, in his opinion, was fortunate:

> . . . the time was ripe for a recession of the mimetic cultural tradition and an advance of the ways of subjectivity. For more

5

> than twenty centuries Western man had
> been exploring the many corners of his first
> great intuition: that things are intelligible
> inasmuch as they are real . . . . Now man's
> second great intuition was struggling toward
> articulation: that all knowledge, and poetry
> in particular, is also personally creative.[9]

It is this recognition of the value of subjectivity which becomes the
primary characteristic of modern art, and although no really radical
application of the idea to the theory of the novel took place until the
twentieth century, implications of such subjective tendencies are
evident in various movements and artistic experimentation of the
nineteenth century, especially during the last few decades of that
century. Just as science at that time began questioning its own
findings, so too did art. The ideas and techniques which we now call
"modern" had not been so codified at that time, but nonetheless, the
seeds of subjectivism, or relativism, as well as the apprehension of
the need for new artistic modes and techniques, were already
present in the late nineteenth century.

The rupture in sensibility and conception of the universe from
the nineteenth to the twentieth century was obviously not as
dramatic as the juxtaposition of the two centuries from our present
viewpoint might indicate. The nineteenth century should be
viewed more as a transitional period in the decline of mimesis, and
the shift in the arts from a strong traditional mimetic impulse to
subjective experimentation was an evolutionary process spanning
both centuries. The search for new techniques by many artists of the
nineteenth century reflects a disillusionment with more conventional manners of representing reality, and, at the same time, a
growing suspicion of the eighteenth century's confidence in the
powers of the mind and values of objectivity. In the works of the late
Symbolists and pre-Surrealists in France (Huysmans, Dujardin,
Nerval, for example), we find implications of the twentieth-century
radical application of the idea of subjectivity. The "radical empiricist"
or "neo-realist" techniques applied to the arts in the twentieth
century, particularly in terms of the novel, were anticipated in the
nineteenth century by artists such as Mallarmé or Alfred Jarry. But

despite these important stirrings, the nineteenth-century novel remained, for the most part, rooted in the conventions of the classical aesthetic.

II

The term "Realism" has become an expedient label applied to a set of literary conventions that propose to represent "real" human experience, and the term is most often used in reference to the movement which arose in the nineteenth century centering around the novel. It was, in part, a reaction against Romanticism, a movement which embodied the idea that the work of art was an idealized representation of life. Although the nineteenth-century novelists protested the improbabilities and sentimentality of romantic art as a distortion or falsification of life, essentially they embraced a rather conservative aesthetic by adhering to a mimetic theory of art which emphasized fidelity to actuality in its representation in literature, and demanded as its materials the commonplace, the average, the everyday. One must agree with Susan Sontag's evaluation of the nineteenth-century novel as the archetypal art form of that century "perfectly expressing that period's wholly mundane conception of reality, its lack of really ambitious spirituality, its discovery of the 'interesting' (that is, of the commonplace, the inessential, the accidental, the minute, the transient)."[10] The nineteenth-century novel focused its attention primarily on the specific action of the immediate and its understandable and probable consequences.

Reality of content, as well as of presentation, is obviously one of the great achievements of the nineteenth-century novel; but at the same time, in its pervasive influence on all subsequent fiction, it has had a restricting and limiting effect on the novel's development.

7

This negative influence is evident in the fact that the modern reader has been trained not only to appreciate such fictional "reality," but to expect it and to apply the term "realistic" in praise of those novels which most closely approximate the models produced in the nineteenth century.

The movement toward subjectivity, which Boyd described, can be seen intensifying in the mid-nineteenth century in the critical writings of Flaubert and later, in James; both writers present novel theory which seriously considers alternatives to the aesthetic of mimesis. Thus, novel theory begins to entertain the idea of an autonomous, subjective presentation of life as a vehicle for realism.[11] It is, however, only in the twentieth century that the ideas of autonomy and subjectivity find expression in their most extreme form and become the primary characteristics of modern art.

The concept of the novel as an autonomous creation, independent of the external, objective world (or at least not entirely reliant on it), reflects the twentieth-century shift in the novel from a public to a private instrument. Until the last quarter of the nineteenth century, reality was, very simply, taken for granted; naturalistic or realistic description rested on the assumption that there was a commonality of perception, as well as on the firm belief that a collective basis exists for the understanding and rendering of human experience. For the nineteenth-century artist, the essential scheme of reality was already created; his task and expertise, to a large extent, lay in his ability to reflect accurately, faithfully, and with some sensitivity perhaps comment upon, human existence. The novel as private instrument in the twentieth century represents a questioning not only of the nature of reality, but also a challenging of the presumed possibility of achieving a definitive conception of it.

The theory of art as autonomous creation also reflects a shift in the twentieth-century novel from the representational to the compositional. Although the content or "world" of the twentieth-century novel may correspond to or approximate the one we know, it is not consciously created to represent anything external to itself. As John Halperin has pointed out, twentieth-century critical views of the novel emphasize "the structure of the work and the symbiosis of its component elements rather than the fiction itself as representative or non-representative of moral or mimetic 'reality.' "[12] Reality, then, in the modern novel, is no longer to be recorded or reflected; rather, it is to be created, hence, the emphasis on composition. The primary concern of many modern novelists has been precisely this process of creation — that is, the relationship of the structural elements within the novel itself. Since the novel cannot continue to mirror the external world in its attempts to present reality, it must itself become the quest which will generate a new reality. The shift in emphasis is from the hope of capturing reality as a phenomenon existing independently of all else, to that of rendering the *process* of discovering reality. And the proliferation of novels-as-quests in the twentieth century is indicative of the modern conception of reality as a potential: a reality which is neither static nor stable, but rather, dynamic and metamorphic. It is in this context that we can appreciate Gertrude Stein's idea of composition as the crucial factor in differentiating past and modern novel writing:

> The only thing that is different from one time
> to another is what is seen and what is seen
> depends upon how everybody is doing every-
> thing. This makes the thing we are looking at
> very different and this makes what those
> who describe it make of it, it makes a compo-
> sition, it confuses, it shows, it is, it looks, it
> likes it as it is, and this makes what is seen as it
> is seen. Nothing changes from generation to
> generation except the thing seen and that
> makes a composition.[13]

In adapting the novel as a vehicle capable of expressing the modern questionings and changing conceptions of the nature of reality, the traditional forms, structures, and techniques which flowered in the nineteenth-century novel have undergone significant transformation. Perhaps the most obvious change in the modern novel is the demise of plot. In the nineteenth-century novel, plot was generally reflective of the belief that events are causally connected; therefore, we find in the novels of that period a

9

definite beginning, middle, and end, as well as a logical progression in terms of probability and time from one event to the next. Obviously, this sort of linear structuring of story becomes meaningless, if not absurd, within the context of a philosophy denying causality. Since, in the twentieth century, one event is not seen as necessarily following from another, *all* events begin to assume equal importance (or the lack of it), and what we are presented with is not a progression but a series of scenes, events, images, organized (if at all) by aesthetic rather than logical concerns.[14]

Another distinction in relation to plot is the very notion of progress inherent in the nineteenth-century concept of the novel. Overall, the century expressed a fairly optimistic belief in human development which is at least suspect, if not denied, in the modern world. The development of character or action which the plot traced implied progress as well as causality. One could assume that the novel's protagonist, by the end of the tale, had advanced in some way: his social position had improved, his integration into his milieu was more complete, or he had achieved a more perceptive understanding or heightened awareness of the meaning of human existence. The novels themselves were often statements or revelations of the "meaning" of life. The modern novel refuses to equate the idea of progress with the idea of better, and tends to avoid intimating any such definitive revelations about life. As Stanley Hyman points out, "where the nineteenth century characteristically saw evolution, we characteristically see only change."[15] This is most likely the basis for the modern artist's tendency to level, to some extent, the events in his or her novel, and at the same time accounts for the modern reader's reaction to these novels as books in which nothing seems to happen.

A further distinction relating to plot is the attitude toward the value of description. In the nineteenth-century novel, description is the vehicle for knowledge. One critic refers to this as the "theory of natural seeing," that is, the idea that perception is uniform and common and one sees what others see by simply looking at the external world, and subsequently, arrives at an understanding of what is "real" or "true."[16] Realism, then, meant the simple process of recording what was seen. In the modern novel, description is either simply an inventory of objects real or imagined, perceived by a particular consciousness, or a vehicle for comprehension rather than knowledge — the fine distinction being that knowledge implies a pre-conceived idea of where exactly reality resides, whereas comprehension implies literally a creating of the world in the act of seeing. What the modern artist comprehends and then describes may or may not be judged definitively as "real," but it is at least an attempt to present a fresh vision, rather than an explanation of or attempt to establish causal relationships between events or between the individual and his universe. The modern novelist expresses a great deal of skepticism about the notion most nineteenth-century novelist assumed *a priori:* man's ability to discover something true about human existence in an entirely objective way, via description of the external world.

As plot, then, in the traditional sense, disintegrates, so too does syntactical form. Sentences and paragraphs, like events, do not necessarily follow from one another. Inasmuch as syntax is an expression of human consciousness, it necessarily follows that the written record of a character's thoughts will resemble the workings of his mind; and, as many novelists in the twentieth century realized, the machinations of the human mind tend to be less logical and lucid than the nineteenth-century novelists supposed (or wished to admit), and perhaps more associative and creative than they cared to recognize. The world, as reflected by the subjective individual human consciousness, is presented in the modern novel exactly as that mind would perceive it and know it: as a complex of memory, sensation, and immediate apperception. Reality, then, at least insofar as it may be sought in the external, objective world, is continually transformed by the perceiving consciousness — the process itself being the catalyst for change in human consciousness which again, in its turn, transforms reality. The process, of course, is continuous; it goes on in this spiraling fashion until consciousness ends. As Erich Kahler has stated, "in penetrating into unexplored strata of reality, consciousness transforms that reality. Thus consciousness changes its world and changes itself." [17]

In addition to plot, another important and perhaps just as obvious change in the modern novel's adaptation to new conceptions of the nature of reality, is the dissolution of time as traditionally conceived. As causality is denied and with it the possibility of delineating beginnings or endings of separate events, the basis for the conception of ordered time disappears. In the modern novel, time is no longer necessarily segmented into past, present, and future, nor is it conceived of as uni-directional. Rather, time is envisioned as it is operative within human consciousness: as flow, as duration, each moment in a person's living a mixture of present awareness and cognition, past memory and association, and future projection and expectation. The modern keynote in regard to time, as Meyer so aptly states, is simultaneity, for "in a world without causation or implication there can be no temporal divisions. Past and future coexist in an all-encompassing, but fluctuating present."[18] Temporal divisions in the modern novel, while expedient, are recognized as arbitrary and subjective; therefore, they are seen as unrelated to the reality of human consciousness. In order to avoid distorting this reality, the modern novel often presents experience within the framework of an eternal present, as for example, in the novels of Franz Kafka.

These important structural and technical transformations evident in the modern novel are indicative of a new orientation to the notion of reality. The anti-traditional and non-representational impulses of the novel in the twentieth century reflect an evolutionary consciousness: the realization that external reality is formed to a great extent by the inner consciousness, since, as modern science has demonstrated, the object of observation is not independent of the observer. At its most basic level, then, the modern novel rejects the possibility of achieving objective representation of external reality; yet, modern artistic endeavor also consciously attempts to construct as well as to destroy. The obvious question is, then, what exactly is it that the modern novel proposes to create? Many critics would still agree with Henry James that "the only reason for the existence of a novel is that it does attempt to represent life,"[19] and in noting the modern novel's refusal to attempt objective representation of reality, would conclude that it lacks art's time-honored *raison d'être.* Such critics would most likely consider the modern novel elitist or destructively insular.

However, modern literary criticism is often, unfortunately, as bound by its tradition as the novel itself has been. The term "realistic" (meaning representative of the external world) has traditionally been applied to novels as a term of praise, while the term "unrealistic" is most often pejoratively leveled at those novels which experiment with new forms and techniques and which are, consequently, most unlike the products the nineteenth century has led us to expect and even to accept as "novels."

Experimental approaches to the novel in the twentieth century, for many writers and theoreticians of the genre, do not simply represent a desire to produce a highly unique creation deriving its value solely from its contrast with more traditional novels, nor do they indicate, as some critics may suppose, a desire to experiment for experimentation's sake. Rather, they represent a reaction to a new philosophical orientation which demands a new medium for its expression. In this sense modern fictional experimentation is a response to new conceptions of the nature of reality, and for many experimental writers, such attempts reflect their commitment to what they consider a very serious enterprise. The novel again becomes the laboratory, the dissecting room, the "instrument of research" as Butor would say, but its objects of observation have changed radically. Now the "subject" is at one and the same time the "object" of creation; that is, the object which is to be rendered does not exist until the author has created it.[20]

Perhaps the hostility evident in much of the negative critical response to serious attempts to create new forms for the novel is the result of the critics' assumption that these contemporary experiments are moving further and further away from reality. The upheaval evident in art today does reflect the deep skepticism it harbors about itself and its role, as well as about human life and culture in general. The equally strong conviction of many critics that modern art is negative, destructive, and dehumanized may stem from their association of the terms "anti-art" or "anti-roman" with the idea of anti-life. Art is, after all, human endeavor, and if one rejects art, as some critics think radical experimentation indicates, isn't one at the same time rejecting the basic impulses of human life? Most of the new experimental novelists would vehemently deny

13

that their work is anti-life or even anti-art, and like Butor, for
example, would defend experimentation precisely because it imitates human life in process, and in so doing, affirms it. As Butor
states:

> La recherche de nouvelles formes ro-
> manesques dont le pouvoir d'intégration soit
> plus grand, joue dans un triple rôle par
> rapport à la conscience que nous avons du
> réel, de dénonciation, d'exploration et
> d'adaptation. . . . L'invention formelle dans
> le roman, bien loin de s'opposer au réalisme
> comme l'imagine trop souvent une critique à
> courte vue, est la condition *sine qua non* d'un
> réalisme plus poussé.[21]

Indeed, it is Butor and some of his disciples who prefer to be called
"neo-realists" rather than "anti-novelists," and who use the term
"neo-realism," rather than "anti-roman," in reference to the new
novel. Their preference for such terminology has implications
similar to those behind Breton's use of the term "surrealism"; that is,
like Breton, they do not mean "away from" the real, but "closer to" or
a "greater" reality.

III

If it is, therefore, a "greater" reality toward which the modern
novel is moving, we must examine those modern novelists who
address themselves specifically to the concept of the novel as search
or research for reality in order to clarify and expand our understanding and appreciation of contemporary experimental fiction.
Two modern novelists whose theories and techniques represent
radical approaches to the novel, and who are concerned specifically

14

with the problem of reality in modern fiction, are Alain Robbe-Grillet and Anaïs Nin. Although there have been other theoreticians of the novel in the twentieth century who have been concerned with reality in the novel, Robbe-Grillet and Nin deserve special attention because both focus specifically on the novel itself as a central element in the creation of fictional reality, and because both evidence a particular interest in the future of the novel. Robbe-Grillet, perhaps the most well-known of the *nouveau roman* writers, has produced novels which are formally and technically original and has written extensively on the theory of the modern novel. His efforts have been paralleled in this country by Anaïs Nin, although her literary reputation has been established more on the basis of her *Diaries* than on her fictional or critical writings. The starting point of both writers' theories of the novel is the conviction that the conventions, methods, and techniques of nineteenth-century realistic or naturalistic novels are inadequate for the representation of modern reality. Their critical writings evidence an overwhelming concern with the distinctions between realism and reality, and with the problems of expressing reality in light of the philosophic and scientific revolutions of the past and present centuries. Both devote considerable time to explanation of their own developing aesthetic as well as to that inherent in the novels of other contemporary experimental writers, and to speculation on the future aims, methods, and forms of the novel as a genre.

An important similarity in their theories is that both envision the novel as a continually evolving form and as an exploration which creates its own significance and reality as it proceeds. As Robbe-Grillet puts it, research is the novelist's task, "une recherche qui se crée elle-même, une recherche qui sécrète elle-même ses propres questions." [22] Anaïs Nin displays equal concern with the novel as search; the search for reality, in particular, is the driving force behind her writings. She has said that it was "to reach a greater reality that I abandoned realism," and that "the emotional reality which underlies superficial incidents is the keynote of my fiction."[23]* Even in the *Diaries* this search seems to be the essential theme,

*Reprinted with permission of Macmillan Publishing Co., Inc. From *The Novel of the Future* by Anaïs Nin. Copyright © 1968 by Anaïs Nin.

15

as Evelyn Hinz has pointed out in her review of Volume IV.[24]

Another similarity in Robbe-Grillet's and Nin's theories is that both have viewed the novel as a synthesizing vehicle for modern artistic and scientific ideas, as well as a dynamic phenomenon which may serve as a catalyst for human transformation. Both also have expressed a belief that the novel of the future will evolve along lines approximating the direction their own fictional products have taken. And in addition, both are concerned with the question of objectivity versus subjectivity in the modern novel.

Although their theoretical approaches to the novel are remarkably similar, their translation of theory into practice has produced uniquely individual results — a phenomenon which indicates that a common view of the problem of reality and its presentation in literature does not necessarily imply a limiting of the individual creative impulses which produce art. If there is a commonality in the developing aesthetic of contemporary experimental novelists, as an examination of Robbe-Grillet's and Nin's theory and fiction reveals, such commonality is not meant to coerce the writer into the sort of conventional product which resulted from the theoretical uniformity in the nineteenth century. In reference specifically to the works of the new novelists in France, however, one can recognize the sort of technical and theoretical uniformity evidenced in the nineteenth-century novel. Although Robbe-Grillet and Butor, in particular, would refute the notion that the new novelists form a "school," the similarity in certain concerns and techniques binds novelists like Robbe-Grillet, Butor, Beckett, Sarraute together, against the Mauriac or Sartre/Camus type of novelist. It would seem, then, that despite their initial intentions, the new novelists in France have created what many critics would call "conventions." Robbe-Grillet's explanation of such "conventions" is that "si un certain nombre de romanciers peuvent être considérés comme formant un groupe, c'est beaucoup plus par les éléments négatifs, on par les refus qu'ils ont en commun en face du roman traditionnel."[25]

However, even in regard to Robbe-Grillet's and Nin's fictional endeavors there are basic similarities: both have attempted to fuse form and content, both present a deliberate architecture in structuring their novels, and both have placed great emphasis on the subjective human perception of the world. Both also seem to have been influenced by surrealism and there is some similarity in their use of techniques, especially the borrowing of effects usually associated with film, and the incorporation of modern scientific knowledge into fictional aims and methods.

What links them above all, however, is their rejection of traditional fictional methods for presenting reality. Their writings are reflective of their awareness of the anomaly of contemporary ideas which often seem to be progressive but are just as often curiously regressive in terms of requirements and expectations of art, especially of the novel. As Anais Nin points out, "we listen to jazz, we look at modern paintings, we live in modern houses of modern design . . . yet we continue to read novels written in a tempo and style which is not of our time, and not related to any of these influences" (p. 29). In proposing a new novel "born of Freud, Einstein, jazz, and science," Nin echoes Robbe-Grillet's concern with traditional theories of fictional reality.

Perhaps the most interesting aspect linking their theories is that both Robbe-Grillet and Nin indicate, in their preoccupation with reality per se, the very crucial but also very traditional critical problem of how art relates to life. In attempting to deal with this problem, not only theoretically but also fictionally, they have expressed a commitment to discovering — or perhaps re-discovering — that there is a relationship between art and life. It is indeed significant that in the latter half of the twentieth century, with two of the most challenging and controversial writers in Europe and the United States, we should find ourselves confronted with the impulses which sparked Aristotle's aesthetic questionings: art and life, the novel and reality.

NOTES

[1]Georges Mathieu, *From the Abstract to the Possible* (Paris: Éditions du Cercle d'Art contemporain, 1960), p. 9.

[2]Eugen Weber, *Paths to the Present: Aspects of European Thought from Romanticism to Existentialism* (New York: Dodd, Mead and Co., 1966), p. 5.

[3]*Ibid.*, p. 11.

[4]Leonard Meyer, *Music, the Arts and Ideas: Patterns and Predictions in Twentieth-Century Culture* (Chicago: University of Chicago Press, 1967), p. 78.

[5]George Steiner, *In Bluebeard's Castle: Notes Toward a Redefinition of Culture* (New Haven, Connecticut: Yale University Press, 1971), p. 138.

[6]*Ibid.*, p. 130.

[7]Michel Butor, *Répertoire I* (Paris: Les Éditions de Minuit, 1960), p. 11.

[8]John Boyd, *The Function of Mimesis and Its Decline* (Cambridge, Massachusetts: Harvard University Press, 1968), pp. 23-24.

[9]*Ibid.*, pp. 302-303.

[10]Susan Sontag, *Against Interpretation and Other Essays* (New York: Farrar, Straus and Giroux, 1969), p. 101.

[11]John Halperin, "The Theory of the Novel: A Critical Introduction," in *The Theory of the Novel: New Essays,* ed. John Halperin (New York: Oxford University Press, 1974), p. 18.

[12]*Ibid.*, p. 18.

[13]Gertrude Stein, "Composition as Explanation," in *Twentieth-Century Culture: The Breaking Up,* ed. Robert Phelps (New York: George Braziller, 1965), pp. 217-218. Stein's essay is not only an explanation of the idea of composition, but a good example of the process as well.

[14]One of the most unique modern innovations in regard to the novel's organization is the possibility for the reader to decide the principles of organization. For example, in Mark Saporta's *Composition no. 1,* pages are unbound and unnumbered, thereby allowing the reader absolute freedom in arrangement. Other examples include Julio Cortazar's *Hopscotch* (the chapters of which the reader

18

may follow in their printed order, in the order suggested by the author, or even in the order dictated by the reader's own sensibilities), and John Fowles' *The French Lieutenant's Woman*, which provides an alternative ending for the reader dissatisfied with the one the author has chosen.

[15]Stanley Hyman, *The Tangled Bank: Darwin, Marx, Frazer and Freud as Imaginative Writers* (New York: Atheneum, 1962), p.428.

[16]Raymond Williams, "Realism and the Contemporary Novel," *Partisan Review*, 26 (1959), 211-212.

[17]Erich Kahler, *The Inward Turn of the Narrative*, trans. Richard and Clara Winston (Princeton, New Jersey: Princeton University Press, 1973), p. 5.

[18]Meyer, p. 167.

[19]Henry James, "The Art of Fiction," in *The Future of the Novel*, ed. Leon Edel (New York: Vintage, 1956), p. 5.

[20]Douglas Hewitt, *The Approach to Fiction: Good and Bad Readings of Novels* (London: Longman, 1972), p. 78.

[21]Butor, p. 9.

[22]Alain Robbe-Grillet, "Nouveau roman et réalité," *Revue de l'Institut de Sociologie*, 2 (1963), 445-446.

[23]Anaïs Nin, *The Novel of the Future* (New York: Collier Books, 1970), pp. 45 & 47. Subsequent page references will appear in the text.

[24]Evelyn Hinz, "Anaïs Nin," *Contemporary Literature*, 13 (1972), 255-257.

[25]Alain Robbe-Grillet, "Révolution dans le roman?" *Le Figaro Littéraire* (March 29, 1958), p. 9.

CHAPTER 2

THE ORIGIN AND PURPOSE OF THEORY

The basis for a comparison of Anaïs Nin and Alain Robbe-Grillet, as I have pointed out, is that both novelists, in writing extensively on the theory of the novel, have evidenced a preoccupation with similar issues: namely, the notion of reality per se, and the related problem of the representation of reality in fiction. In their concern with the modern novel's capacity for reflecting a reality consistent with philosophical and scientific knowledge of the present century, both articulate ideas which not only evaluate prior mimetic theories, but also anticipate the future aims, forms, and directions of the novel as a genre. Although many critics and readers have come to associate both writers with novel theory, neither Robbe-Grillet nor Nin has willingly accepted the role of theoretician of the novel or defendant of fictional experimentation, which many have often assigned to them. Robbe-Grillet states categorically in one of his many essays on novel theory, "Je ne suis pas un théoricien du roman. J'ai seulement . . . été amené à faire quelques réflexions critiques sur les livres que j'avais écrits, sur ceux que je lisais, sur ceux encore que je projetais d'écrire." [1] His sentiments are echoed by Nin, who claims, in her introduction to

The Novel of the Future, that "when I first began to write fiction I had no intention of explaining or theorizing about writing" (p. 1). Despite their reluctance to do so, both have written extensively on the novel, and both have been considered spokesmen for modern fictional experimentation. However, the impetus for such theoretical endeavors was for both, at least initially, adverse critical response to their own fiction.

In Nin's case, the formative roots of her aesthetic theory lay in her defense of D. H. Lawrence, in whose fictional experimentation she found affinities with her own creative inclinations. Attracted to the new literary consciousness and techniques she detected in his writings, she produced what she herself subtitled "An Unprofessional Study" of Lawrence in 1932. Although this study remains essentially an explication and defense of Lawrence's themes and techniques, it is at the same time revealing of her own aesthetic, which as yet had found no outlet in fiction.[2] The eventual synthesis of her ideas into a cohesive critical framework began with this attempt to defend Lawrence and his work, and certain of her key ideas first articulated here were later repeated in a preface she wrote to the first edition of Henry Miller's *Tropic of Cancer* in 1934.[3]

There is a twelve-year span between Nin's writings on Lawrence and Miller and her first critical articles dealing with her own fictional experimentation and developing theory of the novel. During this time Nin launched into her creative writing, first with *House of Incest* (which she termed a "prose-poem"), three novelettes published under the title *The Winter of Artifice* (1938), a collection of short stories, *Under a Glass Bell* (1944), and the novel *This Hunger* (1945), which appeared as Part I of the novel *Ladders to Fire* in 1946.[4] Nin's fiction, like Lawrence's, was met with less than enthusiastic appreciation; she was either neglected by the critics or attacked for her radical experimentation. Therefore, in 1946, she published an essay entitled "Realism and Reality," the purpose of which, as she modestly stated in the first paragraph, was "to clarify some misunderstandings that have occasionally blocked the response to my work."[5] However, the essay goes beyond her stated purpose; it is, first, a defense of her own fictional experimentation, and secondly, a rather sketchy outline of her developing theory, particularly of her ideas regarding the distinction between realism and reality. In addition, the essay was accompanied by a biographical sketch reprinted from *Current Biography* for February 1944, which presents a favorable picture of the author and her published work to date. In 1947 Nin published the second volume of her "continuous novel," *Children of the Albatross*, and that same year published another essay, "On Writing,"[6] which further explicated and defended her fictional theory and practice. It is in this essay that Nin began to develop her ideas on the novel as process, and in which she first used the phrase "novel of the future," linking her fictional experimentation to new trends she detected in the novel form in general. The essay in this chapbook is accompanied by a critical article by William Burford which attempts to define the art of Anaïs Nin to hostile critics. In his essay Burford claims that traditional critical standards and definitions are inadequate for dealing with the kind of fiction Nin was producing, and he proposes that critics "view new writing by new standards."[7]

"Realism and Reality" and "On Writing" are more important for analyzing Nin's theory than are her writings on Lawrence and Miller because they represent her earliest attempts to solidify her ideas into a cohesive theoretical framework and because these ideas now had a firm basis in actual practice. However, her theory, like her fiction at this time, was still in process. As she herself states, as a result of questionings by interested readers and critics, as well as attacks by negative critics, "I found it necessary to solidify my attitude, to formulate a theory" (p. 2). Hence, a book-length study, which she herself labeled "exploratory," appeared in 1968, entitled *The Novel of the Future*. Although Nin claimed in the introduction that the book's purpose was "to study the development and techniques of the poetic novel" and "to evaluate some of the writers who have integrated poetry and prose" (pp. 3-4), the very fact that the study focuses on her own fiction as a basis for discussing experimentation, and further, that it analyzes present tendencies in the novel's direction, allow one to view the study as an exegesis of her own fictional theory. In defending her own experimentation, Nin was forced to defend other experimental approaches to the novel; integrally related to that task was the need to refine and develop her theory of the novel. One wonders if Nin would have synthesized her aesthetic impulses into the kind of cohesive theory eventually expressed in *The Novel of the Future* if, initially, her fiction had been more favorably received by critics.

One might wonder the same in reference to Robbe-Grillet's theoretical writings. As previously mentioned, the initial impetus for Robbe-Grillet's theoretical endeavors was, as it was for Nin, adverse critical response to his own fiction. His first two novels, *Les Gommes* (1935) and *Le Voyeur* (1955), were not, as he tells us, enthusiastically received; indeed, they were violently criticized, and the author was accused of either dehumanizing literature, reducing the novel to an inventory of objects, or exploiting literature by his use of radical techniques. Like Nin, Robbe-Grillet resented the critics' use of traditional novels as yardsticks against which to measure his novels, as well as their application of what he considered archaic critical standards in judging the merit of his work. Consequently, he felt compelled to defend his work, but unlike Nin, the series of articles he produced to "explain" his work to the public and to critics, were never intended to be taken as a cohesive theory of the novel. The impetus for these first critical essays, as he explains it, was that "j'étais persuadé d'écrire pour le «grand public», je souffrais d'être considéré comme un auteur «difficile» " (p. 8). When even these writings were attacked by the critics, and he had responded with a more developed essay, "Une voie pour le roman futur,"[8] published in the *Nouvelle Revue Française,* the results were even more unsatisfactory. Many critics viewed the essay as a "manifesto," and its author as the "theoretician" of what has come to be known popularly as the *nouveau roman.* Further attempts to clarify his ideas were seen by many critics as contradictory; thus, as he explains, "poussé tour à tour par mes recherches personnelles et par mes détracteurs, je continuais irrégulièrement d'année en année à publier mes réflexions sur la littérature" (pp. 8-9).

The key word here is *"réflexions"*; unlike Nin, Robbe-Grillet continued to see his essays on fiction (even though they may often represent further refinement and synthesis of his theoretical notions) as "reflections" rather than "theory." Indeed, *Pour un*

Nouveau Roman, despite what such a title seems to indicate, is simply a selected collection of Robbe-Grillet's critical writings on the novel over the years. Again, in the first essay of that collection, he reiterates his point that he is not a theoretician of the novel: "Ces textes ne constituent en rien que théorie du roman; ils tentent seulement de dégager quelques lignes d'évolution qui me paraissent capitales dans la littérature contemporaine" (p. 9). And although the book lacks the sort of central organizing thesis we find in Nin's work, and is not intended to be a book-length study of the *nouveau roman,* we may, for our purposes, view it as the theoretical equivalent of Nin's *Novel of the Future.*

I

Among the several reasons for viewing *Pour un Nouveau Roman* and *The Novel of the Future* as comparable works, the first and perhaps most obvious is that both display a similarity of origin and purpose. Beyond the common impetus for both novelists' initial theoretical writings which culminated in the two works in question, both writers moved beyond their desire simply to defend their fiction. Both also seemed intensely aware that their fictional experimentation was not an isolated nor unique phenomenon. Neither Nin nor Robbe-Grillet imagined that she/he was writing in a vacuum, nor did either imagine that her/his novels were unrelated to similar experimental stirrings of the time.

Anaïs Nin, for example, who began to write fiction while living in France during the 1930's, was quite cognizant of the impact surrealism was having on the art and artists of her time. Numerous passages in the first two volumes of her *Diary*, which cover the period 1932 to 1939, record her growing awareness and appreciation of the experimentation instigated by the surrealists. She defends the efforts of the surrealists enthusiastically, recognizing her own affinity with them. In one entry, for example, she states:

> I have always believed in André Breton's
> freedom, to write as one thinks, in the order
> and disorder in which one feels and thinks, to
> follow sensations and absurd correlations of
> events and images, to trust to the new realms
> they lead one into. . . . It is not madness. It
> is an effort to transcend the rigidities and the
> patterns made by the rational mind.[9]

And later in the same year she writes, "I have written the first two pages of my new book, *House of Incest,* in a surrealistic way. I am influenced by *transition* and Breton and Rimbaud. They give my imagination an opportunity to leap freely." [10]

Nin was also aware of the impact new psychoanalytic theories were having on our understanding of human perception and the nature of reality, and her long association with Dr. Otto Rank not only brought her into contact with current ideas that were revolutionizing psychology, but influenced her own artistic development as well.[11] Nin's consciousness of her affinities with other experimental writers not only informs, but serves as the basis for many of her critical discussions in *The Novel of the Future.* Throughout she offers critical commentary on numerous writers, including Djuna Barnes, Samuel Beckett, John Hawkes, Franz Kafka, Nathalie Sarraute, and Marguerite Young. Beyond her desire to counter adverse criticism and explain her own aesthetic, Nin displays in *The Novel of the Future* a conscious attempt to "place" her work within an evolving modern approach to the novel form.

Robbe-Grillet displays a similar purpose in *Pour un Nouveau Roman.* Although he disclaims the notion of a "school" among certain writers, he is at the same time aware that his writing is one of

many expressions of a developing consciousness shared by many artists of his time. Although he states that "les nombreuses tentatives qui se sont succédé depuis plus de trente ans, pour faire sortir le récit de ses ornières n'ont abouti, au mieux, qu'à des oeuvres isolées" (p. 15), he is also aware that other writers were facing struggles similar to his own in experimenting with the novel form. For this reason, several essays in *Pour un Nouveau Roman* are analyses of other writers and their works — Raymond Roussel, Italo Svevo, Joë Bousquet, for example — and there are passing references to unnamed "new" novelists throughout. Introducing the set of essays which concentrate on other novelists' work, he explains that he does so to provide examples which will enable him to concentrate on certain themes and forms which herald the "new" novel. He further explains his rationale in the following manner: "Tous offrent . . . quelque chose de profondément actuel; c'est ce quelque chose que j'essaie ici de dégager, et qu'il ne serait pas difficile de retrouver dans la plupart des recherches contemporaines" (p. 69). In his attempt to isolate elements which point to a commonality in contemporary literature, Robbe-Grillet, like Nin, is consciously seaching for affinities among experimental writers in the twentieth century. This shared purpose — that is, to find common denominators in modern fictional experimentation — links *Pour un Nouveau Roman* with *The Novel of the Future.*

An adjunct commonality of purpose is evident from the titles of the two works alone. In their use of the terms "new" and "future" both writers reveal a similarity of perspective. Although they explore primarily the history and current status of the novel form, one senses in both works a sustained excitement and anticipation of further evolutionary trends in the novel form. Throughout their critical writings, both Nin and Robbe-Grillet maintain a view toward the future. In both *Pour un Nouveau Roman* and *The Novel of the Future,* one senses a mood of excited expectancy, an openness to current experimentation which might signal further evolution of the novel form. Their stance is both critical and open; neither implies that the novel ought to move in certain directions, but both are cognizant of tendencies which imply the primacy of certain directions, themes, techniques, over others in the future. Both works, thus, display a critical attitude which in its receptiveness to change and diversity in contemporary fictional experimentation must strike any reader as quite healthy.

II

A second reason for viewing *Pour un Nouveau Roman* and *The Novel of the Future* as theoretically equivalent is that we find in both a similar philosophical premise which is at the root of Nin's and Robbe-Grillet's respective critical approaches. That premise is that the idea of a "theory of the novel," in the sense of a predetermined framework of categorization, is not only impossible, but absurd: impossible because experimentation is and always will take place in the novel, and absurd because, as Robbe-Grillet aptly puts it, "le livre crée pour lui seul ses propres règles" (p.11).

In almost all of his critical essays, Robbe-Grillet asserts his belief that in the world of art, as in the world of human affairs, it is in the nature of things to change. In his view, it is fortunate that many novelists do view literature as a living phenomenon, thereby recognizing that "le roman depuis qu'il existe a toujours été nouveau" (p. 10). Opposed to critics who require consistency in the novel form, Robbe-Grillet denounces the concept of "immutable forms" which necessarily underscores such critical expectations as "consistency" for the novel. To Robbe-Grillet, it is critics with such views who have attempted to establish a pre-determined categorical framework for the novel — as he would say, "un moule préalable pour y couler les livres futurs" (p. 11) — and in so doing, betrayed the very spirit of the novel as an historical phenomenon: an evolving, continually re-newed fictional form. As Robbe-Grillet explains, "Chaque romancier, chaque roman, doit inventer sa propre forme. Aucune recette ne peut remplacer cette réflexion continuelle. . . . Loin de respecter des formes immuables, chaque nouveau livre tend à constituer ses lois de fonctionnement en même temps qu'à produire leur destruction" (p. 12).

The premise that a rigid categorization or "theory" of the novel is impossible also underlies Nin's critical approach in *The Novel of the Future*. Like Robbe-Grillet, she is conscious of the original meaning of the term "novel" as the "new," and it is this meaning which consistently underscores her analysis of the twentieth-century novel. Indeed, she often points out that to demand of the novel certain requirements such as rigid objectivity, realistic or naturalistic description, or consistency of plot and character development as practiced by traditional novelists is "to deprive ourselves of the original intent of the novel derived from the Italian word *novella* — the never-before-experienced" (p. 90). And to her, the outcome of such deprivation is an ossification of the novel form, which of course, would eventually result in the death of the novel. This is not to say that she uses the phrase "death of the novel" in the same way many critics have, or with the kind of implications more conventional criticism has accustomed us to. On the contrary, to Nin, "death" in this sense is simply the decaying of what she conceives of as a very fecund form; when the phrase is applied by many critics to the novel, it is often done so to lament only the demise of traditional novel forms — for example, the realistic or naturalistic novel most commonly produced by nineteenth-century writers. The kind of radical experimentation that Nin applauds in the modern novel is the very thing many critics would point to as a sign of the novel's demise. Nin uses the phrase in an entirely different way, and like Robbe-Grillet, recognizes that the novel is continually "dying" and being renewed, because, as she would explain it, "the creative personality never remains fixed on the first world it discovers . . . never resigns itself to anything" (p. 90). Hence, in line with the continuous evolution of the creative consciousness, the continual evolution of the novel form is always to be expected.

As Robbe-Grillet sees the continual process of degeneration and regeneration operative as a basic law in the novel, so too does Nin. Like him, she believes that each novelist and each novel must "invent its own form," but her understanding of the necessity for such a cycle takes into account certain premises (which we do not find explicitly stated in Robbe-Grillet's writings) regarding the nature of the human personality. In fact, throughout all of Nin's critical essays, one is always conscious of her preoccupation with the artist behind the art; in Robbe-Grillet's work, one often feels that he discusses the novel as if it were a self-generating entity, almost independent of its creator. But this difference, I believe, is more the result of a difference in emphasis in each writer's approach to the discussion of the novel as a form, rather than an indication that either one considers the artist more important than the art.

The basis for Nin's assertion that the novel's evolution is inevitable lies in her belief that man himself is continually evolving. To explain the impetus for the twentieth-century novelist's impulse to experiment with traditional forms, she examines what she terms the "outmoded concept of wholeness" in reference to human life. In the past, wholeness was, she says, "a semblance of consistency created from a pattern, social and philosophical, to which human beings submitted" (p. 193). This produced, she feels, an artificial unity of man which new insights into the relativity of truth and character have dissolved. Recognizing that man is neither a finite nor a static entity, but rather, a fluid being in a constant state of change, he becomes, to the modern artist, the "purest example of relativity." Therefore, Nin claims, novelists must "make a new synthesis, one which includes fluctuations, oscillations, and reactions. It is a matter of reassembling the fragments in a more dynamic living structure" (pp. 193-194).

Nin's emphasis, of course, is on the phrase "living structure"; like Robbe-Grillet, Nin views the novel as a living phenomenon. To deny the novel its perpetual rhythm of renewal and decay — its natural "organic growth," so to speak — would, to her, be tantamount to denying the very impulses of life. And it is for this reason that she continually defends innovation and experimentation in the novel form. As she states in her concluding chapter of *The Novel of*

the Future:
> It does not matter when and where a new
> form begins, but it does matter that we
> should always remain open to innovation.
> . . . it is also natural that the novel should
> change with changes of consciousness. Ex-
> periment and research in the novel are just as
> necessary as they are in art and science. They
> break old molds which can no longer express
> new visions. (p. 193)

Her position is almost identical to Robbe-Grillet's in this regard, for like him, she asserts an *a priori* belief in change as the essential rule in the novel, in reference not only to its history and present mani-festations, but also to its prospective evolution. Both writers, then, stress the idea that the novel must necessarily display an integrity of form if it is to play a fecundating role in the art of its time. As Robbe-Grillet reminds us, "il n'y a pas de chef-d'oeuvre dans l'éternité, mais seulement des oeuvres dan l'histoire; et qu'elles ne se survivent que dans la mesure où elles ont laissé derrière elles le passé, et annoncé l'avenir" (p. 10). The novel, as a vital artistic entity is, in their view, that novel which displays what we might call a "transitional" nature: structurally and thematically couched within its own historical milieu, its roots may dip into the past, but its perspective and its shape are always ushering in the future. Both writers, therefore, would make only one basic requirement of the novel: that its form always remain consistent with the vision informing it — a vision not only emanating from but also reflecting the time and the consciousness of which it is the product.

31

A third reason why we may consider *Pour un Nouveau Roman* and *The Novel of the Future* as comparable theoretically is that both works are informed by the premise that change and evolution in the novel are important not only because they provide for a continually vital or fecund art form, but also because they herald a complementary evolution of man and consciousness. Both Nin and Robbe-Grillet view such an evolution of consciousness as crucial because it can affect the quality of human life. This particular basis for the defense of evolution in the novel reveals an important aspect of each writer's aesthetic: namely, that both assign not only a revolutionary role to the novel and novelist, but a humanizing one as well. In this respect, both writers are integrally linked with the whole of the Western aesthetic tradition, a fact not always evident from a superficial reading of their critical writings, and in Robbe-Grillet's case, a fact often overlooked by critics.

One of the most frequently expressed complaints about Robbe-Grillet's novels has been that they represent or propose a dehumanization of literature. Whether or not the charge has any validity in reference to his novels (an issue which this study does not address), his critical writings provide evidence to the contrary. His defense of innovation rests on the idea that such change brings us closer to, not further away from, a humanized and humanizing literature. Robbe-Grillet expresses his belief in the integral relationship between change in the novel and change in human consciousness when justifying his use of the term *"nouveau roman"* in the essays comprising *Pour un Nouveau Roman*. He explains that he uses the term as a convenient label to denote those writers who are experimenting with new forms for the novel, forms which he defines as ones "capables d'exprimer (ou de créer) de nouvelles relations entre l'homme et le monde" (p. 9). The important point here is that his use of the words *"exprimer"* and *"créer"* as equivalent terms indicates a belief that in the activity of expression lies the activity of creation. To Robbe-Grillet, the "word" does indeed become "flesh"; writers who seek new forms are, in fact, dedicated to "inventing" the novel — an activity, in his view, tantamount to "inventing" man himself. Invention, thus, is a revolutionary act because it implies, in its rejection of old forms in a bid for the new, a desire to transcend the past and create the future, to escape the prison of irrelevancy and align art and mankind more closely to what is germane.

To Robbe-Grillet, such "revolutionaries" of the novel are all too aware that blind adherence to the traditional, with its accompanying resistance to change, can have a dehumanizing effect not only on literature but on all human impulse. As he says, in reference to these "new" writers: "Ils savent . . . que la répétition systématique des formes du passé est non seulement absurde et vaine, mais qu'elle peut même devenir nuisible: en nous fermant les yeux sur notre situation réelle dans le monde présent, elle nous empêche en fin de compte de construire le monde et l'homme de demain" (p. 9).

"To construct the world and the man of tomorrow" might well be considered the aesthetic battle-cry of Anaïs Nin; to a much greater extent than Robbe-Grillet, she defends experimentation on precisely this basis. Her justification of fictional innovation rests on her belief that, at its very core, one finds precisely the sort of humanizing impulse Robbe-Grillet recognized. In *The Novel of the Future,* she often speaks of the "active, fecundating" role of the novelist, a role which she felt had been forgotten or ignored by twentieth-century writers who were producing novels modeled on traditional forms. She labels such writers "passive" and "inert ' and points out that both qualities are antithetical to creativity, to creation.

Nin's use of the term "fecundating" in reference to the novelist's role has to do with her idea that women, in particular, will play a more active role in shaping a new consciousness of the human. It is an appropriate term for her notion of humanization via the novel, for it connotes certain aspects beyond that of "revolutionary." We associate the term with the processes of birth and nurturance, both of which, at least traditionally, have been more commonly perceived as related to the feminine. Humanization, therefore, to Nin, has to do with more than just a new vision; it has to do with the artist's achieving a more balanced vision of the human — a term which has often been used to refer to only masculine experience and consciousness. Naturally, a more "whole" vision of what precisely constitutes the human would be, to Nin, revolutionary.

However, Nin opposes strict adherence with past forms of the novel not only because such forms often express an imbalanced vision but also because, like Robbe-Grillet, she feels this kind of "systematic repetition" of forms is decadent and dangerous: decadent because such rigidity perpetuates — indeed, compels — a corollary rigidity of attitude toward human life, and dangerous because it denies the possibility of human change and evolution. And to her, it was the hope inherent in such evolution which might free mankind from the trap of stasis and transform human life positively in the process. Nin, therefore, also assigns a revolutionary and humanizing role to the "new" novelist, and like Robbe-Grillet, defines this role in reference to the creation of a new vision of man and the world: "The writer acts upon his environment by his selection of the material he wishes to highlight. He is ultimately responsible for our image of the world, and our relation to others" (p. 192).

However, Nin's analysis of the mechanics of this humanizing process in *The Novel of the Future* is developed more explicitly and in greater detail than is Robbe-Grillet's. A major difference between the two in this instance is that Nin discusses the humanizing role of the novelist in psychoanalytic terms, and expresses a view which owes its origin to the ideas on human personality developed by Otto Rank in *Art and Artist* and other works.[12] In her study, Nin explains the ideas she had adopted, particularly her view of the relationship between Rank's ideas and the novelist's role.

> Dr. Otto Rank predicted a new structure of the personality. The writer will be responsible for inventing a form of writing to contain this.
>
> Dr. Rank also said that the artist is primarily an individual who is unable or unwilling to adopt the dominant ideology of his age . . . not because it differs ideologically from his own but because it is collective. For out of his conflict with collective ideas is born the tension which makes us renew our ideas

34

and forms. (p. 192)

It is interesting to note Nin's terminology here; "invent" and "renew" in particular are terms used frequently by Robbe-Grillet, and Nin uses them to express a similar attitude toward innovative fiction.

Another similarity in Robbe-Grillet's and Nin's premise that evolution in the novel inspires evolution on a human level is that for both, the premise rests on the denunciation of what Robbe-Grillet has called the "systematic repetition of past forms." Indeed, their basic rejection of traditional fictional forms not only underlies the whole of their theory of the novel, but also stands as the most obvious factor linking their theories regarding a new representation of reality. This similarity will be discussed in greater detail in subsequent chapters; here it is only necessary to point out its relationship to their specific idea that evolution in the novel form is linked to evolution in human consciousness.

To Robbe-Grillet, the perpetuation of the traditional novel form is dangerous because it "blinds" mankind to the realities of contemporary life, and thus leads to a dehumanization of art. Nin sees the use of the traditional novel form by twentieth-century writers in similar terms; since it is a structure which can no longer adequately correspond to or contain modern reality, it imprisons man in an outdated image and consciousness of himself. Hence, the traditional novel becomes the main target of her attack in _The Novel of the Future._ She condemns what she calls "photographic realism" because "it discounts all possibility of change, of transformations, and therefore does not show the way out of situations which trap human beings," and applauds experimental writers who "keep our dynamism alive by breaking down uniformity, regimentation" and who thus "can rescue man from automatism" (p. 199).

It is important to recognize that both writers' rejection of traditional forms is not the result of an elitist attitude or aesthetic snobbery, but rather, that such rejection stems from their recognition that blind repetition of past forms is potentially dehumanizing. Robbe-Grillet has been accused of deliberately exploiting techniques "which served only to make his novels incomprehensible"[13]; Nin has been accused of being "cultist" or "precious." Yet, neither their theoretical writings nor their fiction warrants such response. As Robbe-Grillet complains, the label "avant-garde" is often used pejoratively in reference to experimental writers and results in the reader's imagining "quelques jeunes hirsutes qui s'en vont, le sourire en coin, placer des pétards sous les fauteuils de l'Académie, dans le seul but de faire du bruit ou d'épater les bourgeois" (p. 26). And Nin reminds us that "labels often alienate a writer from his readers" (p. 190). In their basic theoretical stance, not only in respect to the rejection of traditional novel forms, but to other aspects as well, Nin and Robbe-Grillet are closely aligned. For both would agree with Edgar Varèse that "there is no avant-garde," and suggest instead that in the novel, as in life, there is only change and evolution.

NOTES

[1] Alain Robbe-Grillet, "A quoi servent les théories," *Pour un Nouveau Roman* (Paris: Les Éditions de Minuit, 1963), p. 7. Subsequent page references will appear in the text.

[2] Nin's first fictional work, *House of Incest,* was begun in April of 1932 and published in England in 1936, four years after the study of D. H. Lawrence. The first American edition of the novel did not appear until 1947.

[3] Henry Miller, *Tropic of Cancer* (Paris: Obelisk Press, 1934). Nin's preface was later printed separately by her own Gemor Press (New York, 1947), and is also included in *The Anaïs Nin Reader,* ed. Philip K. Jason (Chicago, 1973), pp. 277-279.

[4] *Ladders to Fire* became the first volume of what Nin later referred to as her "continuous novel," published as a whole by Swallow Press in 1959 under the title *Cities of the Interior.* The other volumes of the continuous novel include *Children of the Albatross* (1947), *The Four-Chambered Heart* (1950), *A Spy in the House of Love* (1954), and *Solar Barque* (1958).

[5] Anaïs Nin, "Realism and Reality," Number 6, *"Outcast"* Chapbooks (Yonkers, New York: Alicat Bookshop Press, 1946), p. 13.

[6] Anaïs Nin, "On Writing," Number 11, *"Outcast"* Chapbooks (Yonkers, New York: Alicat Bookshop Press, 1947).

[7] William Burford, "The Art of Anaïs Nin," Number 11, *"Outcast"* Chapbooks (Yonkers, New York: Alicat Bookshop Press, 1947), p. 5.

[8] Alain Robbe-Grillet, "Une voie pour le roman futur," *Nouvelle Revue Française,* 4 (July, 1956), 77-84. The essay also appears in *Pour un Nouveau Roman,* pp. 15-23.

[9] Anaïs Nin, *Diary,* Volume I, ed. Gunther Stuhlmann (New York: Swallow Press and Harcourt, Brace and World, 1966), p. 11.

[10] *Ibid.,* p. 77. Nin later referred to *House of Incest* as "my season in hell" (p. 289), and sent the manuscript to Artaud for criticism. In addition, certain chapters of the book appeared in the last issue of *transition.*

[11]Several aspects of Nin's fictional theory owe their origin to Rank, particularly to his theory of creativity developed in *Art and Artist: Creative Urge and Personality Development*, trans. Charles Francis Atkinson (New York: Alfred A. Knopf, 1932).

[12]For a summary analysis of Rank's influence on Nin, see Carol Morrell's "Anaïs Nin and the Identity of Women," *Women Speaking*, 4 (1973), 18-20.

[13]Alain Robbe-Grillet, *La Jalousie*, ed. B. G. Garuham (London: Methuen Educational Ltd., 1969); from the "Introduction" to Methuen's *Twentieth Century Texts*, p. xiii.

CHAPTER 3

REALISM AND REALITY IN THE NOVEL

Beyond their basic recognition that the novel displays a continuing evolution as a fictional form, Anaïs Nin and Alain Robbe-
Grillet, like many twentieth-century literary theorists, believe that
the central issue constituting the crisis in the transformation of the
novel in this century has to do with changing conceptions of the
nature of reality. And further, both believe that such conceptual
transformations necessitate the creation of fictional forms congruent
with and appropriate for representing these "new" conceptions of
reality. Although the bulk of modern literary theory posits —
almost to the point of cliché — a belief in the relative and subjective
nature of reality, popular literary production and consumption
contradict such an assertion. The continuing proliferation of novels
which thematically and structurally seem appropriate for the representation of a more traditional conception of reality — that is, the
idea that reality may be definitively and objectively observed and
recorded — attests to this discrepancy between the doctrines of
formalized literary criticism and the tenets recognizable in popular
literary taste. This discrepancy, apparent in the literary contro-

versies and experiments of the late nineteenth and early twentieth centuries, has remained constant up to the present time. It is not surprising then, that both Robbe-Grillet and Nin, in their theoretical writings, display an acute awareness of the discrepancy and address themselves specifically to its significance and the implications which lie behind it. Indeed, it is their recognition of the significance of this gap between formalized literary theory and popular literary taste which accounts for their attempts to construct a more "modern" theory of reality, and to create fictional forms more appropriate to their theoretical views.

I

We may begin to understand Nin's and Robbe-Grillet's theories of reality by first noting that both strongly object to the practice and theory of their predecessors. And it is this primary objection which forms the basis for their eventual rejection of prior mimetic schemes and which compels their attempt to create a new theoretical approach to the mimetic element in modern fiction. Of primary importance is both writers' recognition that the tradition and history of the novel have accustomed writers and readers alike to a particular kind of mimesis which, given the significant philosophical revolutions this century has accommodated, is no longer appropriate. That particular idea of mimesis, as I have pointed out in the first chapter of this study, is characterized in general by the assumption that reality is by its very nature definitive and objective, resides in the phenomenological world, and is collectively recognizable. To both Nin and Robbe-Grillet, then, novel forms displaying this idea of mimesis — that is, forms usually associated with the archetypal nineteenth-century "realistic" novel — are antithetical to the philosophical and perceptual changes which have altered our vision of the world and mankind since that time. And to both writers, the continuing presence of such forms throughout and up to the present time is both cause and symbol of a rigidity of attitude toward experimental fiction.

In introducing their theories of reality, then, both writers note the suspicion with which not only the general reading public, but established literary theorists as well, view new novels which thematically and structurally propose an alternative reality. It is precisely such suspicion and lack of receptiveness to new conceptions of reality which compel both Nin and Robbe-Grillet to call for a more open attitude toward experimental fiction. As Robbe-Grillet, for example, notes, a suspicious attitude toward experimental fiction proposing an alternative reality points to the presence of an established and dogmatic critical system. Indeed, in his theoretical writings, he calls attention to the discrepancy between the claims and practices of traditional literary criticism — a discrepancy which, interestingly enough, parallels the one noted previously between formalized literary theory and popular literary taste. He writes:

> Bien qu'elle [traditional criticism] se dé-
> fende beaucoup de porter sur la littérature
> des jugements systématiques . . . il suffit
> de lire avec un peu d'attention ses analyses
> pour voir aussitôt paraître un réseau de mot-
> clefs, trahissant bel et bien un système. (p.
> 25).

To Robbe-Grillet, these "key words" — *personnage, forme, contenu, vrais romanciers,* for example — constitute a vocabulary which becomes what he terms a "toile d'araignée," at once trapping and holding the novel to an "idée toute faite . . . donc idée morte" (p. 25). Such traps, to him, represent the root problem informing the modern attitude toward the new novel. For this reason he opposes, categorically, the establishment of laws and theories for the novel which, claiming to be of an absolute nature, would eventually coalesce into the hardened system now to blame for the lack of appreciation and acceptance of new visions of reality.

Indeed, Robbe-Grillet declares that it is precisely the struggle

41

against absolute systems for the novel which always bound experimental artists in the past, and which binds together all *nouveau roman* writers today. As he points out:

> Les formes vivent et meurent, dans tous
> les domaines de l'art, et de tout temps, il faut
> continuellement les renouveler: la composi-
> tion romanesque du type XIXe siècle, qui était
> la vie même il y a cent ans, n'est plus qu'une
> formule vide, bonne seulement pour servir à
> d'ennuyeuses parodies. (p. 114)

Wishing to move beyond these "empty formulas," Robbe-Grillet himself consistently avoids making any absolute pronouncements on what a "true" novel ought to be. Rather, he violently opposes what he terms the "schémas préfabriqués" (p. 30) people are accustomed to, which again amount to only a "ready-made" idea of reality. And to him, the task of the new novelist is not, therefore, "à cultiver la ressemblance avec ce qu'il était hier," but rather, as it has always been for the novelist who is conceptually and perceptively functioning in his own time, "à nous avancer plus loin" (p. 115) — in short, to realize and create a new reality.

Anaïs Nin is perhaps even more outspoken than Robbe-Grillet in objecting to the practice and theory of her predecessors, and we find in her writings more frequent references to the inappropriate-ness of traditional mimetic schemes. She denounces, in particular, modern writers and readers who cling to the photographic realism — or what she often terms "reportage" aspects — of the traditional novel in their construction and consumption of modern fiction. For this reason, she calls for a novel of the future which will provide the imagination greater freedom in its expression of what it knows as reality. As she says, "I see in it [the novel of the future] a freedom from boundaries parallel to that claimed by science, a freedom from time, a freedom from geography" (p. 191). And it is her obsessive desire to liberate the novel from all of the tyrannies of rigid fictional formulae which accounts for her condemnation of traditional realists. "The realist" (meaning those who write novels according to the forms and conventions of the nineteenth-century novel) she says, "has been too much of a map maker, tracing roads already in

42

existence. . . . [they] have been eager to reproduce a still, static image rather than a mobile one" (p. 192).

Like Robbe-Grillet, then, Nin takes an equally firm stance against the preconceived notions writers and readers alike hold in regard to the novel, for to her, it is such clinging to worn-out forms which destroys the novel as a fecund, re-vitalizing vehicle for the creation of present conceptions of reality. Indeed, her conception of the process of creativity itself is precisely this escape from conventional patterns — an escape which to her is not executed on the basis of a simple rejection for its own sake, but because, being conventional, such patterns are "dead, used-up" (p. 128). Like Robbe-Grillet, Nin recognizes that "the conventionalities of the novel can no longer communicate what we know,"[1] and she too, therefore, opposes the re-establishment of absolute forms and formulae for the novel. Rather, as she points out, new novel forms are continually evolving.

> . . . when it [fiction] became fixed in a mold, it withered until a new form revivified it. The total death of the novel was always being announced, when what should have been observed was the death of certain forms of the novel. People cling to dead forms. (pp. 155-156)

And it is her ultimate desire to move beyond these dead forms — beyond what Robbe-Grillet would term "empty formulas" or "schémas préfabriqués" — which not only compels her to ridicule, as he does, the popular preference for novels more consistent with traditional notions of reality, but also to condemn those who would establish laws and rigid theories for the novel. "To judge a new French novel, a surrealist novel, a fantasy, an impressionistic happening novel by the same standards applied to the classic 19th-century novel is certainly obtuse" (p. 106), she observes. Yet, she herself would not propose that new standards of an absolute nature be created. Rather, like Robbe-Grillet, she calls for individual freedom in determining the form most consistent with the writer's view of reality. As Robbe-Grillet sees the task of the novelist being simply to "advance beyond" the forms of yesterday and create a new reality, Anaïs Nin sees it as ultimately to reveal, rather than conceal, reality. And to her, it is only via total freedom from restrictive or traditional theoretical notions of what the novel ought to be that the new novelist may reveal, and therefore create, his vision of reality.

The stance, then, which both Nin and Robbe-Grillet assume toward alternative notions of reality and their fictional expression, is impressively liberal. In opposing the establishment of any definitive, absolute forms for the novel, they create a theoretical framework which allows for great individual freedom of choice and expression, yet which, at the same time, proposes a challenging task for the modern novelist: the perfection of the novel form as a vehicle for expressing modern conceptions of reality. It is this very task to which Nathalie Sarraute refers in her theoretical writings on fiction, and it is she, perhaps, who expresses most succinctly the justification for fictional experimentation both Nin and Robbe-Grillet imply in their writings. As she says:

> Isn't it better to try in spite of all the possible obstacles and disappointments to perfect, in order to adapt it to new investigations, an instrument which, perfected in its turn by other men, will permit them to describe in a more convincing, living and truthful manner new situations and feelings rather than to make do with procedures created expressly for grasping what today is nothing but appearance, rather than to tend to strengthen more and more the natural penchant of everyone for deceptive appearances?[2]

Both Anais Nin and Alain Robbe-Grillet would agree that the modern novel could be precisely such an instrument liberating mankind from the prison of false realities.

II

Robbe-Grillet and Nin view the novel not only as an instrument of liberation from rigid and traditional conceptions of reality, but also, as I have pointed out previously, as an instrument of research which creates its own reality as it proceeds. For this reason, we can see that at the very core of their theories regarding the fictional expression and creation of reality, lies an issue which has been basic to all of Western literary theory: the relationship between art and life. Indeed, the bulk of Western aesthetic production can be seen as either an exploration of that relationship or as an attempt to determine precisely what is the nature of the relationship between the "reality" of a work of art and the "reality" existing in and evidenced by the external objective world, as well as the world of human consciousness and endeavor. As Raymond Williams suggests, if we view reality as a continually developing process, we must see the novel as a formative element in that process. "Reality," he asserts, "is continually established by common efforts, and art is one of the highest forms of this process."[3] The emphasis both Robbe-Grillet and Nin have placed on the novel as search attests to their basic agreement with Williams' assertion. Not only do they view the novel as art (and therefore as reality) in process, but both also maintain that that reality is always existent as a potential — that is, to be continually created and recreated throughout time. To them, the novel in itself does not, and indeed cannot, *present* reality; rather, thematically and structurally, it *is* reality. That is, the novel, cast in the form of a search, presents reality in the process of becoming. The modern novel, then, each would maintain, can only construct or create reality; it cannot describe nor, in the strict sense of the term, "represent" reality. As Robbe-Grillet declares, in reference to his own fiction, "Je ne transcris pas, je construis" (p. 139).

An adjunct issue to that of the relationship between art and life has been the relationship between reality and truth, and both Nin and Robbe-Grillet address themselves to this issue also. Historically, mimetic theory seemed to revolve around the assumption that "reality" and "truth" were synonymous terms. In the variety of mimetic schemes, that art which mirrored objective reality was considered "true" art, and the criterion of judgement of whether a particular work was "good" art (and sometimes, whether it was even "art") had to do with its ability to capture such objective truth via faithful reproduction of the world as it was supposed commonly perceived. The trend in modern fiction has been to present reality (as each writer might define it) without, at the same time, claiming to present "truth." And it is in their discussions of the function of art that both Nin and Robbe-Grillet reveal their theoretical affinity with this trend — that is, their belief that the novel, in creating a new reality, is not necessarily at the same time presenting truth.

Robbe-Grillet's well-known and frequently quoted statement — "le monde n'est ni signifiant ni absurde. Il *est*, tout simplement" (p. 18) — implies precisely this modern attitude toward the relationship between reality and truth. Many critics have taken this particular statement as the keynote of Robbe-Grillet's theory and have interpreted it in light of his attitude toward the "signification" he rejects in our traditional approach to literature — that is, his rejection of the process of assigning meaning to objects in the world. As one critic, Stephen Heath, sees it, the statement is Robbe-Grillet's definition of a new theory of humanism. This theory, Heath says, has as its point of departure the idea that literature is a means for breaking down traditional assumptions — and at the same time creating a new awareness — of which aspects of existence may be accurately described as "human." That awareness, he goes on, "is based on the recognition that the world quite simply *is*: it does not *mean* anything, it is just *there*, and any attempt to attach a meaning to it in human terms, to give some 'profondeur' to its solid existence, is dangerously misguided."[4]

However, the statement can be seen to express a more general attitude toward art itself, that being, as a second critic proposes, the idea that "art expresses no *a priori* 'truth' but only itself, and this is sufficient. Art neither imitates nor means nor teaches; it simply is."[5] It is in light of this interpretation that we may understand the statement as an explanation of Robbe-Grillet's attitude toward the relationship between reality and truth. To claim as "truth" one's interpretation of the world would be to assign a particular label, such as "significant" or "absurd" to the world; and although Robbe-Grillet allows for the myriad and contradictory visions each writer has as "reality," he objects to any writer's (or reader's, for that matter) claiming that such personal subjective vision incorporates an absolute truth. For to do so, in Robbe-Grillet's view, would be tantamount to claiming the establishment of an absolute reality. And this, as I have said, is to him antithetical to the very function of the novel.

Robbe-Grillet's idea regarding the relationship between reality and truth is further clarified by his definition of the function of art. He writes:

> Car la fonction de l'art n'est jamais d'il-
> lustrer une vérité — ou même une interroga-
> tion — connue à l'avance, mais de mettre au
> monde des interrogations (et aussi peut-être,
> à terme, des réponses) qui ne se connaissent
> pas encore elles-mêmes. (pp. 12-13)

To Robbe-Grillet then, if the novel does present a kind of truth, it does so not because its author has deliberately set out to achieve that end. Rather, in his attempt to create, construct reality anew, as he knows it, the author has unconsciously set in motion a particular apparatus of questioning which will eventually, and perhaps inevitably, produce answers which the reader may see as "truth."

The premise that reality is not necessarily truth is also evident in Nin's theory, and curiously enough, as with Robbe-Grillet, the premise is most clearly revealed in her definition of the function of art. She assumes, as does Robbe-Grillet, that "the creation of a story is a quest for meaning" (p. 111) and her use of the term "meaning" here we may take as equivalent to the term "reality." In line with this idea and with her view that the novel is always "new," she declares, "It is the function of art to renew our perception. What we are familiar with we cease to see. The writer shakes up the familiar scene, and as if by magic, we see a new meaning in it" (p. 25). Nin, then, sees the novelist assuming a more deliberate role in achieving a new vision of reality than Robbe-Grillet does, since she con-ceptualizes it as a conscious construction of a vision intended to

47

"shake up" traditional views. It is interesting to note her use here of the phrase "as if by magic," for she often conceptualizes the artist's role in creating reality as an alchemical one: as the magician whose illusions (imagination) are so powerful that his audience (the reader) accepts as true what it knows to be un-true, even impossible. Indeed, to Nin, it is in the very nature of "poetry" (a term she uses to designate that pole on the continuum of fictional form which stands directly opposite the pole of "photographic realism") to alchemize the ordinary into the extraordinary. That is, poetry transforms what to her is used-up, dried-out, decadent in the novel into a new reality. As she writes:

> Poetry is the alchemy which teaches us to convert ordinary materials into gold. Poetry, which is our relation to the senses, enables us to retain a living relationship to all things. It is the quickest means of transportation to reach dimensions above or beyond the traps set by the so-called realists. It is a way to learn levitation and travel in liberated continents, to travel by moonlight as well as sunlight.
> (p. 199)

While Robbe-Grillet would see the function of art in what we might call more "mathematical" terms — that is, the creation of an equation balanced by questions which in turn create, then compel, certain answers, *ad infinitum* — Nin sees it in more "alchemical" (or "psychoanalytic") terms. In her view, what the novel can do is revitalize perception by offering an alternative to that familiar schema of reality traditionally imposed on the individual. The novel would offer a truth which in its very nature is liberated and relative: that truth being the reality one sees not only with nightlight and daylight, but also that which lies on the threshold between the two — that is, the reality which in itself is still "in process." The fact that Nin and Robbe-Grillet see both the novel form itself and the reality that form constructs as being "in process," proves the accuracy of one critic's assertion that in the twentieth century, "never has the novel been so thoroughly about itself, yet never has it been so engaged with reality."[6]

In their respective quests for reality, both Robbe-Grillet and Nin recognize the elusive and often contradictory nature of truth (and therefore of reality itself), and take as their *a priori* premise the idea that change is at the very heart of reality. Nin's observation in her study of D. H. Lawrence that "if you go very far all values shift . . . if you are terribly truthful, the ground will always move from under you, and you will have to shift with the constantly shifting truth,"[7] is echoed by Robbe-Grillet's assertion that ". . . alors qu'en vérité *tout change sans cesse* et qu'il y a *toujours du nouveau*" (p. 144).

Robbe-Grillet's and Nin's rejection of prior schemes of reality in fiction and of the notion that truth and reality are equivalent terms, forms the foundation of their theories of reality. For both, this theory develops from their deliberate attempt to distinguish between the conceptual content and implications of the literary terms "realism" and "reality." Indeed, as suggested previously, it is their overwhelming concern with the distinction between the two terms and all that they have historically implied, which reveals the similarity of Nin's and Robbe-Grillet's theoretical stance. At the same time, their distinction serves as the foundation for their ideas regarding the future direction of the novel. And it is this particular distinction with which this chapter is ultimately concerned.

III

As a basis for comparing Robbe-Grillet's and Nin's definitions of the terms "realism" and "reality," I wish to examine those critical essays of each writer which are specifically addressed to an analysis of these concepts. In Nin's case, her two early essays, "Realism and Reality" (1946) and "On Writing" (1947) provide an appropriate starting point. Indeed, the central issue of both essays (as well as of *The Novel of the Future*) is this difference between realism and reality. But it is in the earlier essays that Nin's definition begins to take shape, in the form of a distinction she draws between what she terms "reportage" and "unconscious writing." To her, both terms represent extremes on a continuum she would call "realism" and neither form of writing, she feels, is an appropriate vehicle for the presentation of reality in fiction. At this point, her definition of exactly what constitutes "unconscious writing" is rather vague, but she connects it with what has often been termed the "psychological" novel. As she says:

> Many novels today include the psycho-
> analytical experience. That is only a crude
> makeshift. The novelist knows that psycho-
> analysis has uncovered layers not uncovered
> in the narrative novel . . . . But so far he
> [the novelist] has granted this uncovering
> power only to the professional analyst, not
> realizing that this power must become an
> integral part of his novelist's equipment.[8]

Her rejection of unconscious writing as reality, then, rests on her belief that such writing does not fully integrate the unconscious and the structure it presents in the novel. That is, the unconscious is perhaps used literally (as in its presence in the author's characteri-zation), but it is not incorporated into the novelist's total vision informing the novel. Indeed, Nin claims that the pattern of the new novel will be "one in which everything will be produced only as it is discovered by the emotions: by associations and repetitions, by associate memory . . . by repetitious experiences out of which the meaning finally becomes clear as it does in life," until finally "the pattern of the deeper life . . . will be uncovered and demasked by the writer's process of interpretation of the symbolical meaning of people's acts, not a mere reporting of them or of their words." [9] "Reportage," the other extreme on the continuum of realism, is not reality either, because it remains the mere objective, scientific relating of facts without interpretation, and such factual presentation cannot give the reader the emotional experience she feels is necessary to convey reality. As she says, "nothing that we do not discover emotionally will have the power to alter our vision. In reportage we are once more cheated of experience, and realism is substituted for reality." [10]

Nin sees, then, two extreme forms which fiction has taken historically to present reality; both of these, to her, have failed in their purpose. In her essay "On Writing," her terminology for expressing these two forms has changed, and with that change, there is some clarification of her distinction between the two. "Reportage" she now terms "realism" and "unconscious writing" she labels as "poetry." She now calls for a synthesis of the two forms to produce a fiction one can truly see as expressive of reality. To Nin, the realists have been those novelists who have dealt exclusively with the external drama which emanates from the internal, unconscious drama of the human being; the poets, on the other hand, have been those novelists who have dealt with the emotional reality perceived via the senses. The novelist of the future will synthesize the two extremes, she says, "by following rigorously and exclusively the patterns made by the emotions," to find what she calls the "indigenous structure" in the human unconscious. [11]

To understand fully the distinction Nin makes between realism and reality, it is necessary to understand the basis upon which the whole of her aesthetic rests: the relationship between dream and reality. Indeed, the bulk of her critical work can be seen as a defense of her use of the dream as a basis for the presentation of reality in the novel. In her writings she often quotes Carl Jung's statement, "Proceed from the dream outward" (p. 5) as the keynote of her own fictional intent and practice. As early as 1934, in a *Diary* entry, Nin articulates her belief that the function of art is to capture the reality of the unconscious as presented to the writer in the dream — a reality which to her is more "real" than that known and articulated by the conscious, rational functioning of the mind because it is by its very nature closer to the essence of life: spontaneous, metamorphic, flowing. She writes in June of 1934:

To formulate without destroying with

51

> the mind, without tampering, without kill-
> ing, without withering, that is what I have
> learned by living . . . . *It will become my law*
> *in writing.* All that was pushed into the
> laboratory, dissected under a hospital-naked
> light, pushed into clarity and rationality,
> withered. The beautiful, living and moving,
> dark things that I destroyed in passing from
> nebulous realms of pure dreaming to a
> realization of the dream. Because I did not
> bring into life the same aura of blindness, the
> silences, the same empty spaces, the shreds,
> and the iridescence of images as they appear
> in dreams.[12] [emphasis mine]

Whether or not Nin later actually achieved this goal in her
fiction is a question we need not consider here; it is sufficient only to
note that throughout her long career as a writer and theoretician of
the novel, she held to this concept as the central issue to which her
own and all fiction of the future must address itself. Although many
critics labeled her work as "dreamlike" and "unreal," she
continued to defend her practice and the aesthetic underlying it by
emphasizing, from her early writings through *The Novel of the
Future,* the integral relationship--indeed, the interdependence--of
dream and reality.

Nin uses the word "dream" in reference not only to the images
and drama one experiences unconsciously during sleep, but also in
reference to the "ideas and images in the mind not under the
command of reason" (p. 5), what we often think of as the poetic or
intuitive bursts of perception and awareness. It was, therefore, to
the deeper layers of the human consciousness and psyche that Nin
looked for the wellsprings of reality. As she says, "I felt reality lay at
the bottom of these subterranean worlds" (p. 114), and to her, the
ultimate source of an authentic reality lay within the shape and
significance of the dream.

> The dream was to be the genesis, the
> birthplace of our life. The novels were to be
> the constant description of going into life and

> back into the dream to seek the self when it
> lost its way. In a sense, I continued to say: the
> dream is the key, the source, the birthplace of
> our most authentic self. (p. 120)

And to her, fiction's purpose was to present a recognizable image of man to himself, an authentic self which took into account both the conscious and unconscious aspects of his existence, and which, therefore, presented a more "complete" reality than that evoked by the vision presented in the novels written in a traditionally realistic manner.

Her obsession with the dream in no way indicates a rejection of objective (or what she often terms "surface") reality; on the contrary, she recognized the reality existing in the external, concrete world as a part of the whole human construct which we term "reality." In *The Novel of the Future* she discusses at some length the relationship between surface and unconscious (or "dream") reality, concluding that the objective drama that we see in the world "is a representation, a projection of our inner world into the universal. There is no distinction" (p. 29). The primary emphasis, then, which traditional novelists had placed on the imitation of external reality was, to her, in its extremism and exclusivity, a distortion of what ultimately constitutes the real. This disproportionate emphasis on the external construct of reality, which Nin felt often contradicted the emotional or psychological reality which informs the unconscious and dream life, resulted in novels which presented at best, only a partial reality. Her conviction, therefore, that "the [traditional] imitation of reality creates separation and classifications" (p. 99) accounts for her statement quoted previously that "it was to reach a greater reality that I abandoned realism" (p. 45).

Nevertheless, Nin does accept the necessity of both internal and external reality as a goal in fiction, but she proposes that the writer of the future switch direction. That is, that he begin with the former (internal reality) and move toward the latter (external reality) in approaching authenticity from the framework provided by the dream, for the dream, Nin claims, "instead of being something apart from reality, a private world of fantasy, or imagination, is actually an essential part of our reality which can be shared and communicated by means of imagery" (p. 23).

In following Jung's advice to "proceed from the dream outward," Nin adhered to an aesthetic which stressed the synthesis of the objective and subjective comprehension and presentation of reality. The dream, as she says, is not a "private fantasy" separate from reality; it is, rather, the "birthplace" of reality, the sub-structure or framework which contains the essence, both outline and confine, of the reality we term "life." In using the dream as a vehicle for presenting reality, Nin proposes that it retain its essential nature: the sub-structure, the Ur-pattern containing the archetypal scenario for the drama that becomes each individual's life. The artists's role becomes that of director of this scenario; that is, the novelist takes charge of assigning the meaning to the structure of the dream, then arranges it, orchestrates it to the purposes necessitated by the story he is to relate. Hence, the reality sought by Nin emanates from the dream's structure and content and informs the symbols the writer notes within its content. Therefore, the novelist who would present an entire, complete reality, is the one who first delves into the fecund vision of the dream for his basic fictional content and structure, and then controls and shapes that vision in accordance with the technical and perceptive discipline and techniques of his craft. As Nin expresses the idea in *The Novel of the Future*, "The writing of a novel is, in a sense, a directed dream, embroidered upon a certain theme or thought or sensation" (p. 32). It is this phrase in particular — "directed dream"— which seems to express most aptly the essence of Nin's conception of what the new mimesis should be.

As early as 1933, in a *Diary* entry, Nin articulates her belief in the value of this process for the fictional presentation of reality: "I believe in impulse and naturalness, but followed by discipline in the cutting."[13] While adhering, then, to an aesthetic which stresses spontaneity and inspiration, at the same time, Nin calls for authorial control over that initial vision issuing from the dream material. And it is precisely this idea of "direction" or control over the dream which differentiates Nin's theory from that of the Surrealists.

Although Nin was significantly influenced by the Surrealists and many of their theoretical views regarding fiction,[14] her aesthetic is radically different simply because of her insistence upon controlling the dream material from which the basic structure and content of fiction would arise. She does not believe in simply presenting the dream on its own terms, as it issues unformed and chaotic from the subterranean depths of the human psyche, or as it exists within the human subconscious, or even as it manifests itself in the human imagination and memory. Rather, she believes that the novelist must intervene in his analytical and rational capacity as director, with the raw material which is the dream, and sculpt it into story and significance. The dream, then, alchemized into fiction by the writer/director, does not remain simply "dream," but becomes a fusion of dream and significance. The fictional product represents, therefore, a synthesis of the dream process (similar to that practiced by Breton in *Nadja*) with the rational process usually associated with the construction of any tradtional fictional work.

Nin describes this process in more concrete detail in a passage from the *Diary*, dating from the time she was at work on *House of Incest*, and was most involved with Surrealist ideas and techniques. The passage is interesting not only because it deals with the differences between Nin's and the Surrealists' views, but also because it reveals the basis for her dissatisfaction with and rejection of traditional realistic methods.

> Henry [Miller] was writing about June so realistically, so directly. I felt she could not be penetrated that way. I wrote surrealistically. I took her dreams, the myth of June, her fantasies. But certainly myths are not mysterious, undecipherable.
>
> I see the symbolism of our lives. I live on two levels, the human and the poetic. I see the parables, the allegories. I felt that he was doing the realism, and that I could go up in my stratosphere and survey the mythology of June. I sought to describe overtones. All

the facts about June are useless to my visionary perception of her unconscious self. This was a distillation. But it was not mere brocade; it was full of meaning.

The more I talked, the more excited Henry became. He began to say that I should continue in that very tone, that I was doing something unique, that if anyone was writing surrealism, it was me. Later he dwelt on this. He could not classify my work. It was not surrealism. There was a deeper intention, direction, a more determined attitude.[15]

The "deeper intention" Miller noted in Nin's work was evidently her driving concern to synthesize the two approaches or "processes" of representing human reality — her attempt to avoid, on the one hand, a purely objective "realistic" presentation, and on the other, the "mere brocade" of the "visionary perception" she speaks of in the passage. In short, what Nin calls for is a balance between external and internal reality — that is, a synthesis of the emotional and symbolic experience of the dream and the intellectual interpretation of it. If indeed, as she states, "the richest source of creation is feeling, followed by a vision of its meaning,"[16] then only by such a combination of emotionality and rationality can the artist hope to achieve a complete reality in his fiction. To direct the dream is to practice this very synthesis; and the end result of such a process is the capturing of a reality best described as the spontaneous, metamorphic flux of human life and experience disciplined (and therefore given meaning and significance) by the analytical and critical control of the human rationality.

The crucial distinction then between realism and reality, for Nin, is, as one critic has noted, the difference between two modes of perception: between the conscious and the unconscious, or interior and exterior vision.

Realism is cognitively related to reality, but according to Nin the former is the

partial, the latter the comprehensive expression.
Reality includes the realistic dimension but
goes beyond it. Realism is an end in itself.
Thus, she does not deny the empirical world,
but she considers it as sacramental, that is, an
outward sign of an inward meaning.[17]

And in emphasizing a synthetic, balanced vision of inner and outer
reality, Nin proposes an aesthetic in which reality is a fusion of
dream and interpretation, or appearance and significance. Nin's
view of the novelist of the future is, then, as both dreamer and
realist, for to her, only a sensitivity which can combine both
approaches to the substance and essence of human experience can
produce a fictional work that in the twentieth century can truly be
called mimetic.

IV

Robbe-Grillet's essay, "Du réalisme à la réalité," in *Pour un
Nouveau Roman*, provides an appropriate starting point for an
examination of his analysis of the literary concepts "realism" and
"reality," although it should be noted that the entire collection of
essays in the book have, overall, in Robbe-Grillet's view, a single
unifying purpose related to that analysis: the examination and
definition of the "new realism" which modern fiction, and the
nouveau roman in particular, present. As Robbe-Grillet points out in
a previous essay in the book:

De Flaubert à Kafka, une filiation s'impose

57

> a l'esprit, qui appelle un devenir. Cette
> passion de décrire, qui tous deux les anime,
> c'est bien elle que l'on retrouve dans le
> nouveau roman d'aujourd'hui. Au-delà du
> naturalisme de l'un et de l'onirisme méta-
> physique de l'autre, se dessinent les premiers
> éléments d'une écriture réaliste d'un genre
> inconnu, qui est en train maintenant de voir
> le jour. C'est ce nouveau réalisme dont le
> présent recueil tente de préciser quelques
> contours. (p. 13)

The distinction, then, which Robbe-Grillet makes between realism and reality, is first grounded in a basic distinction between what we might call "old" or traditional realism and what he terms "new" realism. As we have seen, Nin comceptualizes realism as a continuum along which a variety of fictional types (e.g., psycho-logical realism, social realism, poetic realism, "reportage," and "unconscious writing"), each representing a unique theoretical approach to the world and human experience, may be placed. In Robbe-Grillet's theory, however, realism is conceptualized primarily as a convenient label to designate the particular historical manifestations of the accepted and sanctioned (and perhaps most "popular") fiction. Indeed, as Robbe-Grillet puts it, "Le réalisme n'est pas une théorie, définie sans ambiguïté,. . . Le réalisme est l'idéologie que chacun brandit contre son voisin, la qualité que chacun estime posséder pour soi seul" (p. 135). Since Robbe-Grillet discusses the literary concept of realism from an historical perspective, primarily as ideology — as catchword or "un drapeau sous lequel se rangent l'immense majorité . . . des romanciers d'aujourd'hui" (p. 135) — we would do well to examine first the basis for his distinction between older and present forms of fictional realism, before analyzing the relationship he discusses between realism and reality.

To Robbe-Grillet, the primary requirements of literature are that, like all art, it neither serve a pre-established function or purpose, nor uphold or express a pre-existent truth; rather, he says,

58

"il n'exprime rien que lui-même" (p. 42). This particular view of literature may first appear quite revolutionary, but in essence it is not, especially when we compare it to the traditional requirements placed upon the novel — for example, to present an accurate description of the external world, or to present a "slice of life" which is socially, politically, and psychologically perceptive, or to present a particular idea or moral about human experience. Robbe-Grillet continually insists that the new novel cast off the restrictions which false philosophies and ideologies have placed on it, and in stating that the novel ought to express nothing beyond itself, he simply reiterates a point made throughout *Pour un Nouveau Roman* that the novel ultimately creates a world from nothing, from "dust" as he puts it. Yet what Robbe-Grillet sees as the novel's purpose is one numerous theorists and novelists, Anaïs Nin included, have also seen: that literature, basically, should reflect life. "La littérature," he writes, "expose simplement la situation de l'homme et de l'univers avec lequel il est aux prises" (p. 37). If it is, then, man's condition in the world with which the novel has always dealt and must always deal, the ultimate purpose of the novelist is to present man and his world as he, the author, sees it.

It is precisely this point around which Robbe-Grillet's distinction between old and new realism revolves. As he says, just as "tous les écrivains pensent être réalistes," so "c'est par souci de réalisme que chaque nouvelle école littéraire voulait abattre celle qui la précédait" (p. 135). From classicism to romanticism to naturalism to surrealism, Robbe-Grillet points out, the justification informing each movement's or school's creation had to do first with a denunciation of the preceding school's attempt to present reality, and secondly, with the corollary claim that it was most "realistic." The driving aim, then, of all literary revolutions has been, and indeed. Robbe-Grillet recognizes, still is, the search for reality.

> Lorsque une forme d'écriture a perdu sa vitalité première, sa force, sa violence, lorsqu'elle est devenue une vulgaire recette, un académisme que les suiveurs ne respectent plus que par routine ou paresse, sans même se poser de question sur sa nécessité, c'est bien

un retour au réel que constitue la mise en
accusation des formules mortes et la recherche
de formes nouvelles, capables de prendre la
relève. (p. 136)

The continual development of new forms for fiction, which Robbe-Grillet upholds as necessary for the continuing fecundity of the genre, results at one and the same time from the writer's dissatisfaction with the wasteland which formulaic fiction ultimately becomes, and from the discrepancies existing in each writer's idea of what constitutes reality. "Chacun parle du monde tel qu'il le voit," he says, "mais personne ne le voit de la même façon" (p. 136). Since the very essence of life is change, transformation, and since, as he categorically maintains, "L'art est vie" (p. 136), it is to be expected that literary conceptions of "real" life and "real" humanity will continually change. Granting that the world can never ultimately and fully be known, Robbe-Grillet maintains that the novel can do nothing but attempt to develop in accordance with the discovery and re-discovery of man and his situation in the world.

However, "old" realism and its various manifestations in schools and movements represents an ideology which falls significantly short of what Robbe-Grillet recognizes as the ideology inherent in the philosophy of the new novelists. That ideology surmises that first, realism is the explanation or expression of a preconceived and completed reality, and second, that the current or popular movement best expresses that reality. To Robbe-Grillet, new realism expounds a view exactly opposite: that is, that realism expresses a continually evolving reality, and new novel forms reflect not an attempt to achieve a "better" realism, but merely an advancement of realism — an advancement necessitated by the fact that, as he puts it, "Rien n'y est jamais gagné de façon définitive" (p. 136). Because the world changes, because man's relation with the world changes, because human scientific, philosophical, metaphysical, and ethical knowledge changes, "même si le roman ne faisait que reproduire la réalité, il ne serait guère normal que les bases de son réalisme n'aient pas évolué parallèlement.à ces transformations" (p. 137). Robbe-Grillet's major criticism, then, of the various manifestations of old realism is that

60

each, in its turn, claimed to have definitively achieved the most appropriate methods, techniques and ideological basis for representing reality in the novel. And believing that such a goal had been achieved, each rested, in a sense, on its laurels, and became, eventually, a dead formula. The distinction, therefore, between old and new realism has to do with the discrepancy Robbe-Grillet sees in ideological stance. The former, he says, was always a victim of the "illusion réaliste"; that is, traditional realism "emploie le mot «réalisme» comme si la réalité était déjà entièrement constituée," and thus, "réclamerait seulement de la part du roman qu'il respecte la vérité" (pp. 137-138). New realism, assuming that reality has always to do with a subjective, personal perception, maintains "que le roman est justement ce qui la crée"(p. 138). Robbe-Grillet's ultimate defense of new realism, of which the *nouveau roman* is a part, is, therefore, that it endorses the continual renaissance of the novel form as a vehicle for presenting reality, because it recognizes, *a priori*, that art "ne peut exister sans cette remise en question permanente" (p. 136).

Because the prime characteristic of the new novel is, as Robbe-Grillet says, that it conceives of itself as "invention constante et perpétuelle remise en question" (p. 138), it achieves the quality of presentness, which, to him, is the very quality upon which fictional reality is dependent. By being of and in the present — that is, in tune ideologically with man and the world — the *nouveau roman* reveals reality anew, and thereby offers to its readers "une façon de vivre, dans le monde présent, et de participer à la création permanente du monde de demain" (p. 143). Robbe-Grillet's view of the representation of reality in fiction focuses on its cyclic nature; that is, he tends to use "realism" as a general label to describe the formalized, potentially (if not actually) fossilized fictional presentations of reality. To him, art represents reality insofar as it displays the quality of presentness, of timeliness — that it presents a portrait of man and his relationships in the world with a view towards the future yet in a fashion appropriate to the time in which it is written. In this sense, "realism" is a descriptive term for all prior ideologies related to the novel; "reality," on the other hand, de-

Robbe-Grillet's ideas on this new verisimilitude and immediate signification are integrally related. The crucial point he makes regarding verisimilitude is that in the past it was the small detail that "fait vrai" which provided the focus for the novelist in his work. Its quality of "trueness" or verisimilitude resulted primarily from the novelist's act of interpretation; that is, the small true detail was correlated to something outside of the thing itself, was seen as symbol, perhaps, of something larger than itself, was given profound meaning and consequently, assumed a profound significance. It is for this very reason that Robbe-Grillet attacks social realism, because it "reduces" the novel to a meaning (signification) external to it. He criticizes the social realists for viewing the novel as a means for attaining some transcendent value, rather than, as he himself views it, as an end in itself. Indeed, to Robbe-Grillet, : art is all; it is a living form and therefore impervious to what he call the "grilles d'interprétation."

> L'oeuvre d'art, comme le monde, est une
> forme vivant: elle *est*, elle n'a pas besoin de
> justification. Le zèbre est réel, le nier ne serait
> pas raisonnable . . . . Il en va de même pour
> une symphonie, une peinture, un roman: c'est
> dans leur forme que réside leur réalité. (p. 41)

To Robbe-Grillet, this kind of progress practiced by the "old" realists (what we might term "transcendent signification") actually destroyed the fictional world of objects by creating a split between the world which formed the basis for the novel's reality, and the world created by the novel itself. The object, then, ceased to be what in Robbe-Grillet's view it purely and simply was — object — and became a symbolic device or idea. And the world of the novel and its "realness" became then merely a backdrop for allegory, for the presentation of abstract idea, for representation of something external to the novel itself. The ultimate outcome of transcendent signification, as he points out, is that literature

> . . . consisterait toujours, et d'une manière
> systématique, à parler d'*autre chose.* Il y aurait
> un monde présent et un monde réel; le
> premier serait seul visible, le second seul

scibes present fictional endeavor. As he explains it in the essay "Sur quelques notions périmées," the guiding hope of the new novelists was that reality

> ...ne serait plus sans cesse située ailleurs, mais *ici et maintenant,* sans ambiguïté. Le monde ne trouverait plus sa justification dans un sens caché, quel qu'il soit, son existence ne résiderait plus que dans sa présence concrète, solide, matérielle; au-delà de ce que nous voyons (de ce que nous percevons par nos sens) il n'y aurait désormais plus rien. (p. 37)

New realism, as represented by the efforts of the *nouveau roman* writers, is characterized by two interrelated features which Robbe-Grillet feels differentiate it from all prior realisms: its lack of concern for verisimilitude (in a traditional sense), and its attempts to present what he calls an "immediate signification." Because the new novel does not set as its purpose the description of things which existed prior to it, or which exist outside of it, but rather, has as its central ambition the creation of a world which relies on nothing external to it, the new novelist, in Robbe-Grillet's view, no longer describes the world, he *invents* it. He becomes the "créateur d'un monde matériel, a la. présence visionnaire" (p. 141). And that world has, as its primary focus of attention, the object stripped of all meaning other than that which resides in its material presence. In the past, Robbe-Grillet says, things were denied their reality; they were mirrors that simply reflected man back to himself, and as a result, "noyé dans la *profondeur* des choses, l'homme finit par ne même plus les apercevoir" (p. 61) And it is above all the desire to present the world and its objects in a new light, to transform the known and therefore sterile frame of reference man has in the world, and thereby enable him to view the world anew, which accounts for the new novelist's attempts to focus on things, on the object, in a new way. As one critic expresses it, the aim of the new novel is "to transform reality by provoking the reader's consciousness of an experience of existence. This is achieved by a subjective description of objects."[18]

important. Le rôle du romancier serait celui
d'intercesseur: par une description truquée
des choses visibles — elles-mêmes tout à fait
vaines — il évoquerait le «réel» que se cache
derrière. (p. 141)

But to Robbe-Grillet, there is no reality behind or outside of the
object; as the world does not have a transcendent meaning ("Il *est*,
tout simplement"), so too the object ("Il *est*, et c'est tout"[p. 141]).
Recognizing this, the new novelist places reality where, to Robbe-
Grillet, it belongs: in the object, and in the world of objects in the
novel. As a consequence, in the novel, man's relations with the
world are neither transcendent nor symbolic; rather, they are
always direct and immediate. As he says, "Les objets de nos romans
n'ont jamais de présence en dehors des perceptions humaines,
réelles ou imaginaires; ce sont des objets comparables à ceux de
notre vie quotidienne, tels qu'ils occupent notre esprit à tout
moment"(pp. 116-117).

The crux of Robbe-Grillet's theory regarding reality, then,
revolves around his conception of new realism's approach to
signification and his conviction that "C'est sur elle [la signification
immédiate] que portera désormais l'effort de recherche et de
création"(p. 142). Past efforts to achieve fictional reality failed , in
his view, because they all attempted to control the world by
assigning it a meaning. Indeed, the more the world was confronted
and dealt with as signification, the further away the very reality of
that world moved. It is interesting to note in this context that Robbe-
Grillet, like Nin, would view the abandonment of realism as a
necessary step in the attainment of a greater reality. To Robbe-Grillet,
the chief task of the new novel has been to create a literature which
shifts its focus from the "profound" signification of the world and
its objects to the material presence of that world, because to him
"c'est avant tout dans sa présence que reside sa réalité"(p. 22).
Reality, then, is approachable fictionally when the novel abandons
the idea of signification or transcendent meaning as its focal point,
and concentrates instead on the description and evocation of the
object in and of itself.

> A la place de cet univers des «signifi-
> cations» (psychologiques, sociales, fonction-
> nelles) il faudrait donc essayer de construire
> un monde plus solide, plus immédiat. Que ce
> soit d'abord par leur *présence* que les objets et
> les gestes s'imposent, et que cette présence
> continue ensuite à dominer, par-dessus
> toute théorie explicative qui tenterait
> de les enfermer dans un quelconque système
> de référence, sentimental, sociologique,
> freudien, métaphysique, ou autre.(p. 20)

Although Robbe-Grillet stresses the importance of the object in the presentation of reality in the novel, he does not deny the necessity for some sort of interaction of the novelist's imagination in contributing to that creation. Unlike Nin, however, who views the human imagination (and in particular the dream material which issues from it) as a source of reality and calls for authorial control via the exercise of rational, intellectual facilities, Robbe-Grillet views the artist's imagination itself as the controlling and organizing force operant in the creation of fictional reality. The imagination is crucial, he believes, because it is responsible for the creation and selection of the objects themselves. As he maintains, in his essay on the novelist Joë Bousquet,

> Dans le rêve, dans le souvenir comme
> dans le regard, notre imagination est la force
> organisatrice de notre vie, de *notre* monde.
> Chaque homme, à son tour, doit réinventer
> les choses autour de lui. Ce sont les vraies
> choses, nettes, dures et brilliantes, du monde
> réel. Elles ne renvoient à aucun autre monde.
> Elles ne sont le signe de rien d'autre que
> d'elles-mêmes. Et le seul contact que l'homme
> puisse entretenir avec elles, c'est de les
> imaginer.(p. 94)

The contact, then which the novelist makes with the material presence of objects in the world via his imaginative faculties, is what, in essence, creates the reality of the world and its objects in the novel. It is in relation to this idea, then, that Robbe-Grillet condemns the fictional products of "old" realism for their fostering of the "realistic illusion" — that is, of viewing reality as an already completed phenomenon, constituted in the objects residing in the external world. To Robbe-Grillet, it is not the novelist's ability to present the typical or the lifelike detail of the external world which marks him as a new novelist; rather, it is his construction of the "real" object from the product of the external and the imaginary world. Using his own fiction as an example, Robbe-Grillet points out that the gulls he described in *Le Voyeur* emanated ultimately from those existing within his imagination. Admitting that although they probably owed their origin to those in the external world, he maintains that they had been imaginatively transformed, "devenant en même temps comme plus réelles, *parce qu*'elles étaient maintenant imaginaires"(p. 139).

So, like Nin, Robbe-Grillet recognizes reality as more than just fidelity to the objective, external world; indeed, although their theoretical views diverge on their conceptions of the process by which reality is fictionally created, both view reality , essentially, as product of imagination and realism. To Nin, reality issues from the author's synthesis of conscious and unconscious vision, and is, ultimately, the product emerging from the symbiotic relationship of appearance and significance. The object (whether from the dream or the external world) is made "real" by the meaning or inter-pretation assigned by the author. Robbe-Grillet, on the other hand, emphasizes the object's presence rather than its signification, and indeed, denies the importance of what he calls "toute l'âme cachée des choses"(p. 22). Robbe-Grillet claims that we can no longer have any faith in this sort of "depth" — the depth which is, to Nin, the integral element constituting fictional reality — because "la *surface* des choses à cessé d'etre pour nous [le masque de leur coeur, senti-ment qui préludait à tous les] «au-delà» de la métaphysique" (p. 23). In a sense, then, Robbe-Grillet, like Nin, calls for the novelist of the future to be both a realist and a dreamer. But Robbe-Grillet asks the novelist to be realist only insofar as he is measurer, limiter, definer, and describer of the external world, stripped of significance other than that of an immediate sort, and to be dreamer only insofar as he

66

"invente les choses autour de lui" and then "voit les choses qu'il invente" (p. 140).

NOTES

[1] Anaïs Nin, "Realism and Reality," Number 6, *"Outcast"* *Chapbooks* (Yonkers, New York: Alicat Bookshop Press, 1946) p. 17.

[2] Nathalie Sarraute, "Conversation and Sub-Conversation," *The Age of Suspicion,* trans. Maria Jolas (New York: George Braziller, 1963), p. 117.

[3] Raymond Williams, "Realism and the Contemporary Novel," *Partisan Review,* 26 (1959), 212.

[4] Stephen Heath, *The Nouveau Roman: A Study in the Practice of Writing* (Philadelphia: Temple University Press, 1972), p. 75.

[5] John Halperin, "Twentieth-Century Trends in Continental Novel-Theory," in *The Theory of the Novel: New Essays,* ed. John Halperin (New York: Oxford University Press, 1974), p.386.

[6] Peter Brooks, "In the Laboratory of the Novel," *Daedalus,* 92 (1963), p. 277.

[7] Anaïs Nin, *D. H. Lawrence: An Unprofessional Study* (Chicago: Swallow Press, 1964), p. 35.

[8] Nin, "Realism and Reality," pp. 18-19.

[9] *Ibid.,* p. 18.

[10] *Ibid.,* p. 20.

[11] Anaïs Nin, "On Writing," Number 11, *"Outcast"* *Chapbooks* (Yonkers, New York: Alicat Bookshop Press, 1947), p. 26.

[12] Anaïs Nin, *Diary,* Volume I, ed. Gunther Stuhlmann (New York: Swallow Press and Harcourt, Brace and World, 1966), p. 330.

[13] *Ibid.,* p. 167.

[14] Nin's "prose-poem," *House of Incest* (1936), seems to have been directly inspired by surrealist ideas. See Anna Balakian, "The Poetic Reality of Anaïs Nin," in *The Anaïs Nin Reader,* ed. Philip K. Jason (Chicago: Swallow Press, 1973), pp. 11-30.

[15] Nin, *Dairy,* I, p. 130.

[16] Nin, "Realism and Reality," p. 21.

[17] Evelyn Hinz, *The Mirror and the Garden: Realism and Reality in the Writings of Anaïs Nin* (Columbus, Ohio: Ohio State University Libraries, 1971), p. 11.

[18] Emily Zants, *The Aesthetics of the New Novel in France* (Boulder, Colorado: University of Colorado Press, 1968), p. 27.

CHAPTER 4

THE NOVEL AS SEARCH FOR REALITY

Anaïs Nin's and Alain Robbe-Grillet's view of the novel as an evolving form is integrally related to their idea that the novel represents a search or re-search for reality. Their rejection of traditional realism as a viable means for achieving a reality consistent with twentieth-century awareness of man and his relation to the world rests on their belief that such prior fiction conceptualized reality as residing primarily in the external world of human experience and objects, already formed, already realized. Both share the belief that such an approach distorts, rather than reveals, reality. To Robbe-Grillet, the world's reality resides in the presence of things, and the novel's, in its form which takes that presence into account. To Nin, reality issues from the novelist's fictional control of the unconscious and dream material of which the external world is merely a symbol. Both view reality, therefore, as a potential, and both maintain that the novel in itself cannot present or represent reality; rather, thematically and structurally, in its very process of creation, it constructs or creates reality. Both Nin and Robbe-Grillet, like many modern novelists and theoreticians, view reality in creative terms. Both would maintain that if art is indeed imitation, it is so only insofar as it is made, constructed — their emphasis being on the act or process of creation itself, rather than, as it was for prior mimetic schemes, on the act of reproduction or copying (verisimilitude) of human existence. It is in this sense that their theories regarding mimesis are creative; both reject the notion that the novel is a mirror reflecting reality, and posit instead the idea that art is the active shaping of a structure, which in its very form and execution, *is* reality. Both therefore express theoretical views of reality which have their origins in Aristotle's idea of mimesis, but which also suggest some similarity with Bergson's idea that "true reality . . . is an endless becoming, an unceasing flow and flux."[1]

The construction of reality in a literary work is related to the novelist's understanding and expression of human life and experience. And as many modern novelists have pointed out, Nin and Robbe-Grillet included, the essence of experience in the twentieth-century world has been characterized by intense search for meaning, and ultimately, for reality. Such intense philosophical change has resulted in a basic instability in the modern world, which is evidenced by the increasingly problematical aspect of human existence. Reality, as both Nin and Robbe-Grillet have suggested, becomes problematical. It can no longer be taken for granted; the basic assumptions regarding the nature of reality are questioned as the artist attempts to deal with the instability and the continual change and process which characterizes modern life. To communicate this experience, the novel itself, in form and structure, focuses upon reality as it is perceived and experienced *in process*. It is not surprising, thus, given that art is a product of the human consciousness and experience, that the novel (viewed itself as an evolving form and phenomenon) is conceptualized as an integral element in the modern search for reality.

In analyzing Nin's and Robbe-Grillet's views on the novel as a search for reality, it is ultimately the idea of the novel as reality in process which we must take into account. However, there are several related elements of their theory in this particular instance which must also be considered: the idea of the novel as quest, the idea of continuity in the novel, the idea of the novel as a mobile or circular form, and the idea of the novel as invention or re-invention of the world.

I

Both Robbe-Grillet and Nin have emphasized that the impetus for experimental approaches to the novel has been the desire to create a fictional form congruent with and reflective of a modern conception of reality. To both, the novel cast in the form of a quest (perhaps the most archetypal of all Western fictional forms) achieves reality not because the quest form itself is a more realistic one, but because, assuming the structure and design of a search, it presents reality in the process of becoming. The quest, therefore, remains important in the modern novel, but as Nin and Robbe-Grillet have demonstated, it has taken on new meaning and emphasis. The quest is no longer extraneous to the development of plot and character, but rather, it is at one and the same time the plot, the characters, and ultimately, the very form and meaning of the novel itself. Although both Nin and Robbe-Grillet see the form of the modern novel as a quest, their definition of the purpose and

71

format of that quest reveals a basic difference in viewpoint. And that difference is one which revolves around the relationship of the quest to meaning.

As Robbe-Grillet points out, the novel is no longer viewed as a tool for the reproduction of reality; rather, it has relinquished entirely the very notion of itself as an implementation of a predetermined or predefined task. The modern novel, as Robbe-Grillet views it, "ne sert pas à exposer, à traduire, des choses existant avant lui, en dehors de lui. Il n'exprime pas, il recherche. Et ce qu'il recherche, c'est lui-même"(p. 137).

The modern novel's disregard for things outside of itself, in Robbe-Grillet's opinion, has to do with the fact that the novel no longer functions as an intermediary between the world which it is a part of and the world which, in itself, it creates. In the past, the novel played such a role because it was shaped to reflect an already determined construct: that is, a stable, completed, and understandable world. The novelist modeled his creation on that external world and incorporated into the novel's structure the significance he attached to the reality thought to reside in that world of human experience. In the past, the novel's very plot and all the techniques used to develop that plot "visait à imposer l'image d'un univers stable, cohérent, continu, univoque, entirèment, déchiffrable"(p. 31). Indeed, as we have seen, the disintegration of plot in the modern novel is indicative of the breakdown of a stable, consistant conception of the world. The modern novel, according to Robbe-Grillet, does have a story, events, but these "sont sans cesse en train de se contester, de se mettre en doute, de se détruire," and what is lacking, then, in the modern novel, is not a story, only "son caractere de certitude, sa tranquillité, son innocence"(p. 32). The novel, in reflecting the ideological upheavals of the reality of which it is a part, assumes the form of a quest which in its essence is problematical, uncertain, and even contradictory. The reproduction which characterized the essential element of the traditional novel has been replaced in the modern novel by a search for meaning, just as sight (the fictional copying of the world) has been replaced by the vision (the fictional description of objects).

The modern novel cannot, in Robbe-Grillet's view, illustrate a meaning, a signification, "known in advance" because "les significations du monde, autour de nous, ne sont plus que partielles, provisoires, contradictoires même et toujours contéstées" (p. 120). Therefore, the modern novel, in retaining its character of search or exploration, not only explores itself, but also "crée elle-même ses propres significations, au fur et à mesure"(p. 120). To Robbe-Grillet, the modern novelist, denying the validity of any fixed significations and rejecting the idea of pre-determined meanings, can claim to create reality by shaping his novel as a quest, but cannot affirm that this reality has a meaning. The modern novelist can claim only that this reality "aura peut-être un sens après son passage, c'est-à-dire l'oeuvre une fois menée à son terme"(p. 120).

To Robbe-Grillet, the novel cast in the form of a search or quest presents a fundamental way of apprehending reality by the very form it assumes. That form, mirroring the basic process of life in its tentativeness, its uncertainty, and even its ambiguity, achieves reality in a way traditional novel forms do not because it presents reality in the process of being created. The search that the modern novel represents as process is , as Barthes has characterized it, "a search for an intermediary state between things and the world," because, as he suggests, "the *real* is never anything but an inference; when we declare we are copying reality, this means that we choose a certain inference and not certain others: realism is, at its very inception subject to the responsibility of a choice." And it is precisely the modern novelist's relegation of the possibilty of such choice that, to Robbe-Grillet, accounts for his achieving a meaningful creation. The modern novelist does not approach the novel as a means or "tool" to represent a particular thesis or message known in advance; rather, Robbe-Grillet insists, "c'est précisément ce «comment», cette manière de dire, qui constitue son projet d'écrivain"(p. 121). And even though the writer's enterprise is, as Robbe-Grillet maintains, more "obscure" than any other, and its fictional manifestation as search may present a reality perhaps more obscure than that presented by traditional novels, it is, nevertheless, an enterprise which to him promises a more viable approach to the meaning and significance of our experience. For the novelist, released from the trap of a fixed reality — the "grilles d'interprétation" Robbe-Grillet often speaks of — is now free to explore and create his own world, his own reality via the exercise of fiction. To do less, Robbe-Grillet maintains, would be to perform a useless exercise.

> Le romancier ne prétend pas apporter une signification nouvelle qu'il aurait découverte, mais rechercher une signification qu'il ne connaît pas lui-même encore. . . . Mais si l'écrivain connaissait lui-même à l'avance ces significations-là, je crois que son oeuvre serait nulle, qu'il serait tout à fait inutile qu'il l'ait écrite.[3]

The novel-as-search, therefore, provides a format by which man may approach the meaning of the world and human experience, for as Robbe-Grillet maintains, "ce sont les formes qu'il [l'homme] crée qui peuvent apporter des significations au monde"(p. 120).

Like Robbe-Grillet, Nin views the novel as an evolving form and views modern fiction as the continuous process of establishing reality. Indeed, Nin stresses the importance of the *process* of the work of art as the integral element in reflecting life and in achieving reality. Nin too castigates the traditional novel for its view of reality as *fait accompli* which the novel has simply to reflect like a mirror. To Nin, art and life are integrally related in the movement, the dynamic elements, and the process of flow which underlie both; the task of the modern novel is not to capture a pre-existing construct, but to reflect life as it is experienced. "I do not accept ready-made patterns," she writes in the *Diary;* "I do not practice the accepted integrations, the familiar synthesis. I am evolving a more fluid, flowing life, living out each fragment, each detour without concern for the conclusions."[4]

It is precisely this quality of reflecting life as it is experienced in process which attracted Nin to D. H. Lawrence's fiction, and it is, first of all, in her analysis of Lawrence's fictional innovations that Nin began to articulate the kernal of her aesthetic: the idea of the novel as process. "Lawrence has not system," she writes, "unless his constant shifting of values can be called a system: a system of mobility. To him any stability is merely an obstacle to creative livingness." To Nin, the basis of Lawrence's fictional creation rested on this "system of mobility," which emphasized what she termed "oscillation," the quality of change and evolution which Nin saw reflected in life. The value of Lawrence's work, she felt, lay in its awareness that reality was not static, and its attempt to translate this awareness into art by presenting experience as a fluid, meta-morphic, and constantly shifting configuration, reshaping itself as life in its cyclical process is continually reshaped. As Nin says in her study of the novelist: "Life is a process of becoming, a combination of states we have to go through,"[6] and to her, if the novel is to reflect life, its very design must take this process into account.

Nin, Like Robbe-Grillet, rejects the conventional novel which, in its artificiality, its static qualities, offers the reader what she terms "ponderous, premeditated designs"(p. 126) which conceal con-temporary reality. To Nin, the most fecund design of the modern novel is the quest, but unlike Robbe-Grilet, who sees no pre-determined object of inquiry for the novel, Nin proposes a focus for its search: "the quest of the self through the intricate maze of modern confusion." Nin's view of the design of the quest is more precise and focused, but not substantially different than Robbe-Grillet's, for like him, she views the quest as a viable format for the novel by which man can achieve some understanding of his experience. Just as Robbe-Grillet rejects the traditional novel's image of a stable, coherent, and "decipherable" universe, Nin rejects its image of a finite, static, unified self. Man, she says,

> . . . is fluid, in a constant state of flux,
> evolution, reaction and action, negative and
> positive. He is the purest example of relativity.
> We as novelists have to make a new synthesis,
> one which includes fluctuations, oscillations,
> and reactions. It is a matter of reassembling
> the fragments in a more dynamic, living
> structure.(pp. 193-194)

What Nin proposes as a model for a "more dynamic, living

structure" is the design and organization of the inner world — the world of the unconscious, the dream — because, ruled as it is by change and flow, it reflects life. To Nin, this inner world is usually in opposition to the surface, external world used by the conventional novel as the substance of reality. Since to her the goal of the quest is the delineation of the authentic self, it is appropriate that the modern novel present a structure which is reflective of the environment of that self. What is most interesting, however, is that she compares that design of the inner world to jazz, a musical structure or composition which is characterized particularly by the qualities of improvisation and spontaneity.

> It is unwritten music in the sense that it is constantly improvising: it is ruled by free association of ideas and images. Most of it is clear to the intelligence, but extremely perceptive and audible to the emotions. This was the sign of its (the inner world's) authenticity: if it came from the hidden sources it touched our feelings.[8]

Nin's reference to jazz is particularly revealing of her aesthetic. Jazz is a musical form which creates its own discipline within its spontaneity. A basic theme or thread sits at the center of the composition, around which variations are woven. Its nature is spontaneous and as performance and product it remains less under the demands of tradition than of inspiration. Its ultimate source lies in the emotions rather than the intellect and, therefore, its expression remains integrally related to and issues from mood tempered by an intellectual translation of sensations, impressions, and feelings. By its very nature it reflects flow, metamorphosis, and is therefore, always "unfinished." Jazz, thus, as a form characterized ultimately by process, is a particularly appropriate image for Nin's conception of the design of the new novel, since its design is intensely dynamic and live. Indeed, Nin believes she has endowed her own fiction with these qualities, and often describes her own process of fictional creation as "musical" or "poetic," by which she means that she follows the design of music or poetry in constructing reality. "I have composed by following and obeying the dictates of life rhythms and moods, by an excresence of words, by attrition, by accumulation, by organic cellular growth of both ideas and feelings, obeying above all the laws of spontaneity and enthusiasm."[9] And in the Preface to her "continuous novel," *Cities of the Interior*, she claims, "I have never planned my novels ahead. I have always improvised on a theme."[10] In referring to this particular work in *The Novel of the Future*, she explains her own process as being one which, like life itself, was cumulative and organic. "I began an endless novel, a novel in which the climaxes consisted of discoveries in awareness, each step in awareness becoming a stage in the growth like layers in trees"(p. 123).

Nin, like Robbe-Grillet, sees the novelist's task as ultimately an obscure one; and like him, she indicates a belief in the novel as a search for something not yet known to the novelist. She too would assert that the novel cannot illustrate a meaning known in advance, but she feels that the design of the novel, the quest, moves it toward a meaning or illumination of reality. And Nin, perhaps more than Robbe-Grillet, believes in the novelist's responsibility for his own creation and the novel's responsibility to its audience in expressing significance. "In a confused world the novelist has a great responsibility not to add to the confusion," she claims, for "depicting chaos without any illumination of its meaning is adding to chaos"(p. 36). That meaning, for Nin, issues from the synthesis of the inner and outer drama depicted by the novelist, and ultimately has to do with a revelation of man's authentic self to himself. "The creation of a story is a quest for meaning," she asserts; "the objects, the incidents, the characters are always there . . . but the catalyst is the relation between the external and internal drama. The significance of this relationship *is* the drama. The meaning is what illumines the facts, coordinates them, incarnates them" (p.111). Nin, unlike Robbe-Grillet, would affirm that the reality which issues from the design of the quest has a meaning. That reality, to her, is composed of accumlative "discoveries in awareness" which, as a continuing process, reveal man to himself. The meaning of the quest is both contained in the design itself (insofar as that design reflects the essence of life as a process of becoming) and revealed in its product, that is, the novel and the portrait it reveals of the authentic self. And to Nin both avenues toward meaning or significance are dependent upon each other, for, as she points out, "you cannot reach unity and integration without patiently experiencing first of all all the turns of the labyrinth of falsities and delusions in which man has lost himself."[11]

The novel-as-quest or search, then, to Nin, provides the form which Robbe-Grillet feels can "attach significations" to the world. To her, it is perhaps the most fecund, and certainly the most appropriate, form for achieving a reality consistent with our experience and knowledge of twentieth-century existence. As a design which both incorporates and reflects the idea of process, the novel-as-quest presents reality in the process of becoming. To Nin, life is characterized above all by its fluidity, its shifting, oscillating, metamorphic nature; and man, as a part of the life process, is fluid also. In creating an authentic portrait of the self, the novel must take that fluidity into account, which it can do, Nin believes, via the design of the quest: "The closer we come to creating that feeling [of flow] in our work, the closer we come to what life is, which is constant change and openness and evolution."[12]

II

In viewing the novel as a search for reality which takes the basic design of the quest as both symbol and technique of search or research in process, Nin and Robbe-Grillet emphasize the necessity for a fictional form congruent with that conception — a form which is essentially continuous and which is perhaps best characterized as "mobile" in Nin's case, and "circular" or "revolving" in Robbe-Grillet's. The idea of the novel as a continuous process is inherent in the idea of the novel as a search. Both Nin and Robbe-Grillet see the quest as essentially open-ended and, therefore, as an appropriate design for the new novel, which itself is conceived of as an open form, a work continually "in progress."

Nin's conception of the novel as a continuous form originates in her lifelong practice of diary-writing. The diary is, above all, fluid; it has no beginning, middle, or end, and is characterized primarily by freedom of movement and theme. Nin's ideas on the shape of the new novel, her view of reality as process, and indeed, her own fictional experimentation, were influenced by her experience with the diary form. To her, the living quality such writing evidences results from its attempt to synthesize the inner and outer conscious-ness and experience of the writer, while allowing for the continual possibility of change and evolution. As she says in reference to her own fictional process, "Synthesis, integration, are often replaced by absolutes. There is no danger of dogmatism in the way I work, only in conventional summaries, not in the open, indefinite continuum I practice."[13] Perhaps the most important aspect of the form she proposes for the novel is that its development be organic, via the process of accumulation and synthesis, rather than via an imposed, linear, progressive structuring of details, which necessarily culminates in summary and in a static, completed, and closed fictional world.

The importance of the diary form in shaping Nin's ideas on the form of the novel cannot be underestimated. Like the diary, the novel, Nin would assert, should be continuous only because such a free-flowing form is capable of capturing human experience in the process of becoming. In her discussion of the relationship between diary and fiction, Nin focuses on the quality of continuity whose fostering she attributes to the diary.

> The diary, creating a vaster tapestry, a
> web, exposing constantly the relation be-
> tween the past and the present, weaving

meticulously the invisible interaction, noting
the repetition of themes, developed the sense
of continuum of the personality instead of
conclusions or *resolutions* which were in-
validated by any recognition of the relativity
of truth. This tale without beginning or end
which encloses all things, and relates all
things was a strong antidote to the incoher-
ence and disintegration of modern man. I
could follow the real patterns and gain insights obscured in most of the fragmentary or
superficial novels with their artificial climaxes
and resolutions. (p. 159)

To write with a view toward conclusion or resolution is, to Nin,
antithetical to the idea of the novel as a search for reality, for the
validity of the search rests finally in its tentativeness, its probing
quality which is continually shaping and reshaping experience as it
is discovered. To resolve or end the quest is to enclose the fictional
world in a kind of stasis which is not an accurate construction of
reality. As we have observed, Nin maintains that reality cannot be
expressed in a static form, for its very essence is ultimately constant
movement, process, which in its very expression is continually re-
formed and transformed. The artist's goal is to capture, as Nin feels
D. H. Lawrence did, the living quality of experience, the living
essence of human consciousness and vision of the world. Only a
form, therefore, which is organic is suitable for capturing this
"livingness." And to Nin, "form is created by the meaning, it is born
of the theme. It is created very much as the earth itself is
created . . . . It is organic development."[14]

When she calls for fluidity and spontaneity in the novel form,
Nin is not simply reiterating surrealist aesthetics. Her idea of
continuity takes into account two processes: the spontaneous
expression of the dream and unconscious, as well as the critical
exercise of the rational faculties. "The two processes are necessary,"
she asserts, "letting the unconscious flow but then knowing how to
select what is significant, important, meaningful."[15] To Nin, it is the

conventional novel whose form is characterized by a pre-dominance of critical selection and rational discipline. That form is not continuous in the sense Nin proposes; rather, it is represented by a linear progression of details, facts, events, culminating in a conclusion or summary. This hardened design presents a closed fictional universe, a universe that to Nin is "dead," unorganic, and incapable of achieving reality. Continuity, to Nin, has to do with the openness, the freedom of the novel's form; the novel can be a composition which is self-contained, but which also allows for additions and deletions. In this sense, the novel is not "continued"; it is simply on-going, as life itself is, and it has no pre-determined starting point or concluding point. As one critic has explained, Nin's idea of continuity is circular; that is, the novel represents a cycle with no fixed beginnings or endings, a cycle that in Nin's own fiction expresses emotional states and human relationships in an ever-changing continuous process. Therefore, the essential element in the novel as a continuous form is "circularity or total immersion in the moment of time."[16]

Integral to Nin's idea of continuity is that of time as a succession of moments reflecting the fragmented and transfigured process of reality. If the novel is to achieve "livingness," fluidity, Nin says, then the novelist must "capture the living moments"(p. 160). Nin proposes that the novel (which to her seeks to delineate the authentic self) be composed of moments charged with intense emotionality "because they are the moments of revelation." She goes on to explain that the novelist's focus should be on the "heightened" moment because "it is the moment when the real self rises to the surface, shatters its false roles, erupts, and assumes reality and identity"(p. 160). Nin believes that in capturing these intense moments in her fiction she reaches a greater reality of feeling and the senses. Although the novel which focuses on these revelatory moments may at first appear formless and discon-tinuous, it creates, as a composite, a true reality. "The novelist," Nin claims, "decomposes elements and recomposes them to create another truth"(p. 63), and in this sense, the artist constructs a mobile, a freely-turning construct in space and time which, depending upon the particular area of focus, presents a world which is continually changing, continually revealing reality. The idea of the novel as a continuous creation, a mobile in space, is made possible by Nin's concept of the self as "a mobile turning in space, the space of experience and other people."[17]

The basic material of the mobile is the raw experience of life; its angles and shapes, or configuration, are formed by the artist's control of that material. Certain elements are stressed, certain details are focused in on, placed in a more prominent position. As Nin explains it, "A concentrated lighting thrown on a few critical or intense moments will illumine and reveal more than a hundred details which dull our keenness, weary our vision"(p. 26). In the same manner, the novelist discards the familiar, the thousands of details which were thought to guarantee the traditional novel its reality. The image evoked may be deliberately incomplete, Nin says, so that the reader is forced to concentrate on a new element, for the role of the artist is "to seek to renew and resharpen our sense by a new vision of the familiar."[18]

The continuous form that Nin proposes for the novel is a mobile one in both senses of the term: first, it is ever-changing, flowing, creative, and at the same time, it is a construction which is free-floating within its own fictional space. It neither begins nor ends, but in its movement presents the bits and pieces of the human psyche and experience which together compose reality. The ultimate control of its movement and shape rests in the artist's focus on the "living moment," much in the same way the camera focuses upon a particular spot. The mobile form, therefore, enables the novel to achieve a greater reality because in its continuity and selected focus on the living moment it matches what Nin conceives of as the way we truly see, in images resembling film sequences. As Nin explains it, the novel as a mobile construct forces the reader to concentrate on new elements, new designs of life experience, so that "the lens of this camera eye, our subjective vision, each time catches new aspects, new territories of experience. That is what I call the adventure of reading, the research, the innovation."[19]

To Robbe-Grillet also the ultimate goal of the new novel is to research so as to reveal "new territories of experience," or as he would say, to search for new forms "capables d'exprimer (ou de créer) de nouvelles relations entre l'homme et le monde"(p. 9). The novel-as-quest is precisely such an attempt, for it presents a fundamental way of apprehending a new reality by its very design. For Robbe-Grillet, the fictional form most congruent with the conception of the novel as a search for reality is one which is continuous (in the sense that it is always evolving) and one which is essentially creative and inventive. "Chaque romancier, chaque roman," Robbe-Grillet states, "doit inventer sa propre forme" (p. 11); the word to be emphasized here is "invention."

A significant element in Robbe-Grillet's rejection of the traditional novel is his conviction that its form was an adoption of a ready-made, hardened, and lifeless mold. The very basis of his defense of experimental fiction is that it represents an attempt to move beyond the essentially futile and absurd representation of reality inherent in the archaic form of the traditional novel. Indeed, to him, the repetition of past forms of the novel is not only futile, but dangerous, for it locks the novel into a universe which is closed, static, and basically inhibitive of evolution. His objection to past novel forms centers around his conviction that they are formulaic, rather than inventive. For the new novel, he asserts, "la forme est invention, et non recette"(p. 43-44). It is, therefore, always open, continually evolving, and like life itself, an expression of reality in progress.

To Robbe-Grillet, form is not only motion (in the sense of a continuous invention, construction), but is itself the expression of reality, for it is the form of the novel which "constituera . . . le monde particulier de l'écrivain"(p. 41). Even though the reader may be unable to define precisely and definitively its meaning, that particular vision of the world constitutes reality. The "content" of the novel, to Robbe-Grillet, cannot be separated from its form; rather, the new novel proposes a more intimate relationship of content and form. As Robbe-Grillet points out:

> Parler du contenu d'un roman comme
> d'une chose indépendante de sa forme, cela

> revient à rayer le genre entier du domaine de
> l'art. Car l'oeuvre d'art ne contient rien, au
> sens strict du terme (c'est-à-dire comme une
> boîte peut renfermer, ou non, à l'intérieur,
> quelque objet de nature étrangère).(p. 42)

The form no longer serves simply as frame, or "envelope" as Robbe-Grillet puts it, enclosing the universe of the novel's content; rather, the content of the new novel is essentially the construction of a reality in process and its form is the fictional vehicle whereby the continuity of the content is assured. In this sense, the content no longer takes precedence over the form, as a receptacle for significance, the function it served in the traditional novel. As Barthes points out, the modern novel reveals the fusion of content and form, Indeed, its structure is like an onion, "a construction of layers (or levels, or systems) whose body contains, finally no heart, no kernal, no secret, no irreducible principle, nothing except the unity of its own surfaces."[20]

The form, therefore, which Robbe-Grillet proposes for the new novel is perhaps best characterized as "circular," and is explained most clearly in relation to his ideas on time and description in the new novel. As he points out, the function of description in the traditional novel was to delineate the general design of the setting and to highlight the most important aspects of that setting. In the new novel, description serves a different function: "elle ne parle plus que d'objets insignifiants, ou qu'elle s'attache à rendre tels. Elle prétendait reproduire une réalité préexistante; elle affirme à présent sa fonction créatrice"(pp. 126-127). The creative function which form now displays rests precisely in its quality of circularity — that is, the role of form is to keep the content of the novel in motion, in process. As Robbe-Grillet points out, the primary interest of description is not "dans la chose décrite, mais dans le mouvement même de la description"(p. 128).

What ultimately characterizes that movement is what Robbe-Grillet refers to as its "paradoxical" nature. Such description *seems* to be inventing its object, but in its process of mobility it cancels out its object by repetition, by contradiction, by correction, and by shifting the reader's focus on it. Finally, "lorsque la description prend fin, en s'aperçoit qu'elle n'a rien laissé debout derrière elle: elle s'est accomplie dans un double mouvement de création et de gommage" (p. 127). The "double movement" may be paradoxical, as Robbe-Grillet says, but it is also circular or revolving because it continually returns (albeit from a different angle or perspective) to the object of focus in a continuing present. As one critic explains it:

> Form once depended upon . . . a linear cause and effect construction, but the concepts . . . of cause and effect have become untenable and have been replaced by relationships. Form, therefore, depends upon a radiation of relationships from the point of a continuing present. This mobilizes the reader's perspective of the world, permitting him to pass from one relationship to another without rendering reality stationary.[21]

This revolving form, Robbe-Grillet says, is ultimately a construction of moments, and the new novel presents itself "sous la forme de déroulements temporels"(p. 130). Therefore, the new novel's treatment of time is also characterized by the paradoxical movement of destruction following upon construction. The role of time in the traditional novel, Robbe-Grillet points out, was perhaps a more important one than it presently is. Time "completed" man, he says, "il était l'agent et la mesure de son destin." In the modern novel, time appears extraneous to its temporality: "Il ne coule pas. Il n'accomplit plus rien"(pp. 133).

Time and description in the new novel, thus, reveal the circular quality of form (its continual movement) and illustrate the new approach to reality which the new novel attempts. In its circularity the new novel reveals reality as it is in process: the continuous construction and destruction of the object of attention. As Robbe-Grillet points out, the finest works of contemporary writers

> . . . ne prétendent à aucune autre réalité que celle de la lecture, ou du spectacle, mais

> encore elles semblent toujours en train de se
> contester, de se mettre en doute elle-mêmes à
> mesure qu'elles se construisent. Ici l'espace
> détruit le temps, et le temps sabote l'espace. La
> description piétine se contredit, tourne en
> rond. (p. 133)

As description turns in circles, creates and then destroys the object in focus, it also destroys the reader's "confidence" in the object, and makes of the novel a succession of present moments. This present "s'invente sans cesse" via the processes of repetition , modification, and denial, and therefore, never displays the "accumulation" of objects or facts which was characteristic of the traditional novel and which, to Robbe-Grillet, accounted for its "story."

The new novel proposes no such story in the sense of a movement towards conclusion or summary which reveals reality; rather, the very approach to movement and continuity is tentative and contradictory. Like Nin, Robbe-Grillet would assert that the novel cannot achieve reality by assuming a form which allows for conclusion or resolution. To do so would be to render an already completed, closed world, rather than a world in the process of being created. And to Robbe-Grillet and Nin, the novel itself is the instrument whereby reality is discovered or constructed, not simply the container for a pre-conceived reality. The novel as a search for reality does not present a copy of reality, but makes a composition of significant or heightened moments which in their continual genesis reveals the nature of reality as a continually evolving process. Indeed, this new form of the novel, Robbe-Grillet points out, is an invitation for the reader himself to participate creatively, to "inventer à son tour l'oeuvre — et le monde — et d'apprendre ainsi à inventer sa propre vie"(p. 134).

86

NOTES

[1] As quoted by J. B. Priestly, *Literature and Western Man* (New York: Harper and Brothers, 1960), p. 306.

[2] Roland Barthes, "Literature Today," *Critical Essays* (Evanston, Illinois: Northwestern University Press, 1972), pp. 159-160.

[3] Alain Robbe–Grillet, "Nouveau roman et réalité," *Revue de l'Institute de Sociologie,* 2 (1963), 445-446.

[4] Anaïs Nin, *D. H. Lawrence: An Unprofessional Study* (Chicago: Swallow Press, 1964), p. 14.

[6] *Ibid.,* pp. 39-40.

[7] Anaïs Nin, "The Writer and the Symbols," *Two Cities,* 5 (1969), 37.

[8] *Ibid.,* pp. 39-40.

[9] *Ibid.,* p. 35.

[10] Anaïs Nin, "Preface,"*Cities of the Interior* (Chicago: Swallow Press, 1959), p. vii.

[11] Nin, "The Writer and the Symbols." p. 37.

[12] As quoted by Priscilla English, "An Interview with Anaïs Nin" (September, 1971), *A Casebook on Anaïs Nin,* ed. Robert Zaller (New York: New American Library, 1974), p. 194.

[13] Nin, *Diary,* V, pp. 112-113.

[14] Anaïs Nin, "On Writing," Number 11, *"Outcast" Chapbooks* (Yonkers, New York: Alicat Bookshop Press, 1947), p. 27.

[15] Anaïs Nin, "The Craft of Writing," *A Woman Speaks: The Lectures, Seminars and Interviews of Anaïs Nin,* ed. Evelyn Hinz (Chicago: Swallow Press, 1975), p. 213.

[16] Sharon Spencer, "Introduction," Anaïs Nin's *Cities of the Interior,* (Chicago: Swallow Press, 1974), p. xiii.

[17] *Ibid.,* p. xix.

[18] Nin, *Diary,* V, p. 55.

[19] *Ibid.,* pp. 55-56.

[20] Roland Bartes, "Style and Its Image," in *Literary Style: A Symposium,* ed. S. Chatman (New York: Oxford University Press, 1971), p. 10.

[21] Emily Zants, *The Aesthetics of the New Novel in France* (Boulder, Colorado: University of Colorado Press, 1968), p. 54.

CHAPTER 5

THE FUTURE OF THE NOVEL

In the twentieth century, particularly in the last several decades, the modern novel has been characterized by radical experimentation which seems to be moving the novel towards what theorists like Alain Robbe-Grillet and Anaïs Nin would call a "new" or "greater" realism. As this study has demonstrated, the basis for a comparison of the two writers' theories lies primarily in the fact that both have addressed themselves specifically to the concept of the novel as a search for reality. In their theoretical writings, as well as in their fiction, one may look for the impulses of this trend toward neo-realism in the belief that an examination of each writer's aesthetic will expand our understanding and appreciation of contemporary experimental fiction. An adjunct basis for comparison is that one may find in their writings strong evidence of a commonality in the developing aesthetic of experimental fiction which, judging from the highly unique creations of each writer, allows for great formal and technical freedom. One notes, thus, in Robbe-Grillet's and Nin's theories, a common view of the problem of reality and its construction in the modern novel. In attempting to synthesize and compare the theoretical bases revealed in their writings, one may also hope to develop a more coherent framework for understanding and evaluating experimental trends in the future. This study has attempted to analyze those common elements in the theory of both writers by examining their views of the use and purpose of novel theory, their distinctions between the literary terms "realism" and "reality," and their concepts of the novel as a search for reality.

Perhaps the most important aspect underlying both Robbe-Grillet's and Nin's theoretical views on the construction of reality in modern fiction is their interest in and speculation on the future development of the novel. Indeed, their theory seems constructed and articulated with a view toward the future. The very impulse of their theoretical writings is their *a priori* recognition that the novel itself is an evolving form and that such evolution is the manifestation of an impulse to establish a new and more intimate relationship between art and life. The commonalities which underlie their views on the future evolution of the novel and its form are to be found in three major areas: first, an optimistic conviction that the future evolution of the novel will produce a form reflective of a truer reality; second, the belief that the novel of the future will be a dynamic form serving as a catalyst for human transformation; and third, a belief in the novel's continuing evolution as a free form for human expression. It is these three aspects held in common by Robbe-Grillet and Nin which mark their theories as basically humanistic.

I

Both Robbe-Grillet and Nin are optimistic about the present experimentation in the novel form because they feel such experimentation is centered in a commitment to the freedom of artistic expression. Indeed, it was precisely the lack of such freedom which accounted initially for their rejection of traditional novel forms and the ideology supporting these forms. Their stance is essentially anti-authoritarian; both would free the novel from the narrow strictures of the past, from the confines of the novel's own historical roots. Their rejection of traditional novel forms springs not from a desire to bolster their own experiments, but rather, from a belief that art is only vital when it can transcend the prison of its own origins and evolve in accordance with the changes which have affected all of twentieth century life. Both feel, therefore, that the requirements that once governed the conventional novel are no longer relevant in reference to an imaginative process springing from and reflecting a twentieth-century consciousness.

Both Robbe-Grillet and Nin, thus believe that any predetermined requirement for art is antithetical to the basic impulses of the human imagination, which is the source of all art. And both hold that view even in reference to their own theories. As Anaïs Nin puts it, "I do not expect my conclusions to be finite or dogmatic. . . . I do not believe in finite, absolute statements. I am leaving it to the new writers to explore all the possibilities, to experiment with their own potentialities"(p. 191). And Robbe-Grillet too claims that his reflections are not to be considered absolute statements on the new novel, for, as he admits, "nous ne savons pas ce que doit être un roman, un vrai roman; nous savons seulement que le roman d'aujourd'hui sera ce que nous le ferons, aujourd'hui, et que nous n'avons pas à cultiver la ressemblance avec ce qu'il était hier, mais à nous avancer plus loin"(p. 115). For both, the rationale behind fictional experimentation and literary theory should be freedom of expression and development. And indeed, both writers have attacked not only the proliferation of out-dated novel forms, but the biases of those critics and readers who support only such traditional products. As Robbe-Grillet points out, the literary system itself is heir to a tradition which necessitates opposition to new experimental forms. New forms, he says, are "unconsciously" compared to and judged by reference to "consecrated" forms: "Le nouveau-ne balbutiant sera toujours considéré comme un monstre, même par ceux que l'expérience passionne"(p. 17). Writers and critics alike, he feels, must free themselves from their preconceptions and conventions regarding the novel, for the world "refuse de se plier à nos habitudes d'appréhension et à notre ordre." (p.20).

Robbe-Grillet's optimism regarding fictional experimentation results from his conviction that such endeavor will free the novel and man from what he calls the "tyranny of significations." Nin has a similar rationale for supporting fictional experimentation; as she says, "Each new experience requires a new form of expression"(p. 170). But unlike Robbe-Grillet's, Nin's optimism has more to do with her belief in the artist's power to transform our knowledge and understanding of the world and human experience than with the experimental nature of his products. "The novelist is, after all, but a gauge of what is happening, a mirror," she says. "He can articulate what is not yet visible to the unobservant eye"(pp. 74-75). Nin believes that the artist possesses great and perhaps prophetic perceptive powers, and via the exercise of his skill and intuition, can "Light up with his expression worlds which may never have been lighted before"(p.170).

Both Nin and Robbe-Grillet also share the conviction that radical experimentation is necessitated by the present state of the art, which both would characterize as stagnant and inert. Indeed, Robbe-Grillet claims that the art of the novel has so deteriorated that "on imagine mal que cet art puisse survivre bien longtemps sans quelque changement radical" (p. 16). However, neither believes that such deterioration necessarily implies that the novel form is dying. While Robbe-Grillet withholds judgement on the issue by asserting that only history will reveal "si les divers sursauts que l'on enregistre sont des signes de l'agonie, ou du renouveau" (p. 16), Anaïs Nin affirms that the experimental novelists (whom she calls the "research workers" of literature) are keeping the novel form alive.

> In literature, we should not always read the books blessed by the majority. This trend is reflected in such absurd announcements as the 'death of the novel,' . . . when we know that these are continuous trends which evolve and merely change form. The suppression of inner patterns in favor of patterns created by society is dangerous to us. Artistic revolt, innovation, experiment should not be met with hostility. They may disturb an established order or an artificial conventionality, but they may rescue us from death in life, from robot life, from boredom, from loss of self, from enslavement.[1]

The basis for both writer's optimism is ultimately the potentialities which experimental fiction holds out for the future. Nin's hope for the future is that it may see the establishment of a new synthesis of the interior and exterior consciousness which will enable the novel to achieve a greater reality. "We are now in an intermediate period," she claims. "There has been a chasm between poetry and prose in which writing lost its magical power, a chasm between art and science, and a chasm between the conscious and the unconscious. These will one day be fused"(p. 165). Robbe-Grillet is hopeful simply because he recognizes a continuing process of death and rebirth in the novel form, a process which, he believes, will be as evident in the future as it has been in the past. This evolution is characterized by a rejection of traditional values as irrelevant, and the establishment of new and more appropriate values which, in their turn, will become the targets for future criticism and bases for future experimentation. He writes:

> . . . les oeuvres nouvelles n'ont de raison d'être que si elles apportent à leur tout au monde de nouvelles significations, encore inconnues des auteurs eux-mêmes, des sig-

93

nifications qui existeront seulement plus
tard, grâce à ces oeuvres, et sur lesquelles la
société établira de nouvelles valeurs . . .
qui de nouveau seront inutiles, ou même
néfastes; lorsqu'il s'agira de juger la littérature en train de se faire.(pp. 123-124)

II

Robbe-Grillet's and Nin's optimistic view of the novel of the
future is integrally related to their belief that the evolution
evidenced by experiment with the novel form is a manifestation of a
drive to establish a new and more intimate relationship between art
and life. That new relationship hinges, ultimately, on a return to the
human as the central focus in the novel. As Robbe-Grillet explains,
"le nouveau roman ne s'intéresse qu'à l'homme et à sa situation
dans le monde"(p.116). Indeed, a truly revolutionary aspect of the
nouveau roman, which he points out, is that it proposes a return to
reality by abandoning the outdated concept of the novelist as the
objective observer and reproducer of an absolute, fixed, and certain
reality. What Robbe-Grillet refers to is a return to the subjectivity
which characterizes the human consciousness — the subjectivity of
the individual human vision through which the world is revealed. It
is this quality which Barthes recognizes in Robbe-Grillet's own
experimental fiction. With Robbe-Grillet, Barthes says, the novel
      . . . becomes a direct experience of
man's surroundings, without this man's being
able to fall back on a psychology, a metaphysic,
or a psychoanalysis in order to approach the

94

objective milieu he discovers. The novel, here, is no longer of a chthonic, infernal order, it is terrestrial: it teaches us to look at the world no longer with the eyes of a confessor, a physician, or of God — all significant hypostases of the classical novelist — but with the eyes of a man walking in his city with no other horizon but the spectacle before him, no other power than that of his own eyes.[2]

And Robbe-Grillet sees this focus on the human as a crucial element underlying the *nouveau roman* in general. As he says, "C'est Dieu seul qui peut prétendre être objectif. Tandis que dans nos livres, au contraire, c'est *un homme* qui voit, qui sent, qui imagine, un homme situé dans l'espace et le temps, conditionné par ses passions, un homme comme vous et moi"(p. 118). The *nouveau roman* reports one man's experiences which, like all human experience, remains limited, uncertain, and contradictory because they are presented with the subjectivity characteristic of man's true vision of himself and his world. The author forsakes the unreality of a god-like stance and represents only himself and his limited human vision; as a result, according to Robbe-Grillet, "c'est un homme d'ici, un homme de maintenant, qui est son propre narrateur, enfin"(p. 118). Anaïs Nin echoes this view by claiming that experimental fiction gives a direct vision of emotional, subjective reality. By giving form to inward experiences, by objectifying the subjective, the novelist makes these experiences conceivable and possible to the reader, who may then understand better his own inner life.

In viewing the novel as a search for reality, Nin and Robbe-Grillet propose that its function be to involve the reader in the process of the quest. Because in its very movement the novel creates rather than represents a fixed reality, it invites the reader to participate in the search for and discovery of reality. In so doing, it involves the reader in the very process of life as becoming, as well as in the production of a relevant meaning for that process. As Nin sees it, the writer's ultimate responsibility is "to increase, develop our senses, expand our vision, heighten our awareness and enrich our articulateness."[3] Because the new writer views his role primarily in reference to the reader, sees himself assisting the reader in understanding and developing his own vision of life and experience, the new novel, she feels, "could point the way to all the potentialities of life, of mediums, of art" (p. 169). To Robbe-Grillet, the new novel also expands human vision because both novelist and reader cooperate within its structure to continually invent and re-invent reality. As he says,

> ... loin de le négliger, l'auteur aujourd'hui
> proclame l'absolu besoin qu'il a de son
> concours, un concours actif, conscient,
> *createur*. Ce qu'il lui demande, ce n'est plus de
> recevoir tout fait un monde acheve', plein, clos
> sur lui-même, c'est au contraire de participer à
> une creation, d'inventer à son tour l'oeuvre—
> et le monde—et d'apprendre ainsi à inventer
> sa propre vie. (p. 134).

This particular dynamic between reader and text is important because it will not only assure a human focus in the novel, but also, Nin and Robbe-Grillet feel, may enable the novel to fulfill a primary task in human life; to serve as a dynamic catalyst for human transformation. It is precisely this opportunity for change which Nin sees as the primary quality of experimental writing — a quality which to her results from the novelist's optimistic view of human life. "He doesn't despair," she says. "He doesn't say . . . nothing can be altered. Instead, the artist has always said: 'Although the world is like this . . . I can change it.' "[4] To her, the novelist changes the world by his exploration of the nature of reality and, specifically, by his concern with depicting the intimate relationship between the individual's inner consciousness and external experience. "Good exploratory writing shows you the man of tomorrow, the man you might be, based on psychological probabilities. There is no way to become familiar with this new world within ourselves except by a fearless exploration of it" (p. 169). If, as Nin claims, the experimental novelist believes that life is changeable, that it can be metamorphosed, then he will, in his fiction, once again assume an active, fecundating role. He will assist the reader in achieving personal transformation by presenting not only what is, but what can become reality. To her, the novelist's true role should be not simply to "depict man as he is but also as he might be. He [the novelist] is there to give an example of the freedom of choice, freedom to transcend his destiny and his surroundings, master his limitations and restrictions" (p. 174).

Robbe-Grillet is more tentative than Nin in his assessment of the effects of the new novel on human life, but like her, he asserts that the novel can indeed effect change. While he believes that the reader, forced to cooperate with the author in the construction of reality, learns in the process to invent the work, the world, and his own life, at the same time, he recognizes the difficulties such involvement may present to the reader. Even these, however, Robbe-Grillet sees as a vital part of the creative process. The difficulties not only increase the reader's understanding of the process of perceiving reality, they also allow him a vision of the openness of the world and the reality being constructed. In this way, the novel helps the reader to envision the potentialities of the world in which he exists. "Si le lecteur a quelquefois du mal à se retrouver dans le roman moderne, c'est de la même façon qu'il se perd quelquefois dans le monde même où il vit, lorsque tout cède autour de lui des vieilles constructions et des vieilles normes" (p. 116). The new novel, therefore, intimately acquaints the reader with the very experience of change. But the greatest benefit of the new novel to man lies in its strict adherence to a presentation of things through the shifting, subjective human point of view, which in its exploratory nature mitigates against the application of "une grille d'interprétation périmée" that to him would conceal rather than reveal reality. Indeed, he claims that all readers can recognize the world in which they live and their own thoughts in the new novel; therefore, the new novel "au lieu de les tromper sur une prétendue signification de leur existence, les aideront à y voir plus clair" (p. 119).

For both Robbe-Grillet and Nin, experimental fiction is dynamic because it holds out to man the possibility of a new vision of himself, his experience, and his world. In its emphasis on the subjective, ideologically-unencumbered construction of reality, which not only focuses on the individual but also engages him in the process of creation, it offers a means whereby man may once again make sense of his own existence, not as a *fait accompli,* but as an on-going, potentially changeable phenomenon. If the reader can re-invent himself, Robbe-Grillet and Nin would maintain, he can also re-invent the world.

In their speculation on the future of the novel and, indeed, informing all of their theoretical views on experimental fiction, both Robbe-Grillet and Nin recognize the need for a basic freedom in the evolving and developing form of the novel. In their defense of fictional experimentation, as well as in the practice of their own art, they express the same commitment to the freedom of the imagination in constructing the reality of life as the individual human consciousness knows and experiences it. In their view of the future of the novel, both Robbe-Grillet and Nin are optimistic that the transformation evidenced by the exploratory and highly experimental novel forms' in the twentieth century will again manifest themselves, as the human imagination continues to go beyond its own knowledge of life, to break free of the artistic prisons of convention and tradition, and to transcend its own construction of reality. Nin's claim that "there is a trend in the novel now which is trying . . . to get back to the basic reality of experience . . . in order to be revitalized,"[5] lends weight to Robbe-Grillet's assertion that such new fiction "non seulement est désormais possible, mais en train dèjá de voir le jour," and his prediction that "elle va représenter, — en s'accomplissant — une révolution plus totale que celles d'où naguirent, jadis, le romantisme ou le naturalisme" (p. 16).

For indeed, if the novel continues its search for a more vital and intimate relationship between art and life, it will attain that "greater reality" which many writers and critics have seen as the basic impulse in fictional experimentation. The significance of Robbe-Grillet's and Nin's theories of the novel is that they reveal a trend which rejects the idea of art in the twentieth century as a luxury or "cultural frill," and which, therefore, offers some hope for those concerned with the gap that currently exists between art and life. The aesthetics expressed by Nin and Robbe-Grillet are truly revolutionary because they reveal an evolving consciousness which heralds not the dehumanization of art that many critics feared, but rather, the renewal of a commitment to fictional experimentation which centers itself within contemporary life and experience as it is lived in process.

NOTES

[1]Anaïs Nin, *Diary*, Volume V, ed. Gunther Stuhlmann (New York: Harcourt Brace Jovanovich, 1974), pp. 49-50.

[2]Roland Barthes, "Objective Literature," *Critical Essays*, trans. Richard Howard (Evanston, Illinois: Northwestern University Press, 1972), pp. 23-24.

[3]Nin, *Diary*, V, p. 171.

[4]Anaïs Nin, "Read College Commencement Address," in *A Woman Speaks: The Lectures, Seminars, and Interviews of Anaïs Nin*, ed. Evelyn Hinz (Chicago: Swallow Press, 1975), p. 3.

[5]Nin, "Conversation with Deena Metzger," in *A Woman Speaks: The Lectures, Seminars and Interviews of Anaïs Nin*, p. 200.

BIBLIOGRAPHY

Albérès, René. *Histoire du roman moderne*. Paris: Éditions Albin Michel, 1962.

_____. *Metamorphoses du roman*. Paris: Éditions Albin Michael, 1972.

Ames, Van Meter. "The New in the Novel." *Journal of Aesthetics and Art Criticism*, 21 (1963), 243-250.

Aristotle. *Poetics*. Trans. S. H. Butcher. New York: Hill and Wang, 1961.

Auerbach, Erich. *Mimesis: The Representation of Reality in Western Literature*. Trans. Willard R. Trask. Princeton, New Jersey: Princeton University Press, 1953.

Balakian, Anna. *Literary Origins of Surrealism*. New York: New York University Press, 1966.

_____. *Surrealism: The Road to the Absolute*. New York: Noonday, 1959.

Baldanza, Frank. "Anaïs Nin." *Minnesota Review*, 2 (1962), 263-271.

Barnes, Hazel. "The Ins and Outs of Alain Robbe-Grillet." *Chicago Review*, 15 (1962), 21-43.

Barthes, Roland. "Littérature littérale: Alain Robbe-Grillet." *Critique*, 20 (1955), 820-826.

_____. "Littérature objective: Alain Robbe-Grillet." *Critique*, 18 (1954), 581-591.

_____. *Writing Degree Zero*. Boston: Beacon Press, 1967.

Beardsley, Munro. "On the Creation of Art." *Journal of Aesthetics*, 23 (1965), 291-304.

Becker, George. "Realism: An Essay in Definition." *Modern Language Quarterly*, 20 (1949), 184-197.

Berenson, Bernard. *Aesthetics and History*. New York: Doubleday Anchor Books, 1954.

Bergonzi, Bernard. *The Situation of the Novel*. London: MacMillan, 1970.

Bersani, Leo. *Balzac to Beckett: Center and Circumference in French Fiction*. New York: Oxford University Press, 1970.

Blanchot, Maurice. "D'un art sans avenir." *Nouvelle Nouvelle Revue Francaise*, 5 (1957), 488-498.

Block-Michel, Jean. "The Avant-Garde in French Fiction." *Partisan Review*, 25 (1958), 467-471.

Bocheński, J. M. *The Methods of Contemporary Thought*. Trans. Peter Caws. Dordrecht, Holland: D. Reidel Publishing Co., 1965.

Brodin, Pierre. *Présences Contemporaines: Écrivains Américains d'Aujourd'hui.* Paris: Nouvelles Editions Debresse,.1964.

Brombert, Victor. *The Intellectual Hero: Studies in The French Novel 1880-1955.* Chicago: University of Chicago Press, 1961.

Brown, E. K. *Rhythm in the Novel.* Toronto, Canada: University of Toronto Press, 1950.

Cocking, J. M. "The 'Nouveau Roman' in France." *Essays in French Literature,* 1 (1965), 1-14.

Cohn, Dorrit. "Castles and Anti-Castles, or Kafka and Robbe—Grillet." *Novel, A Forum on Fiction,* 5 (1971), 19-31.

Collins, Robert. *The Novel and Its Changing Form.* Winnipeg, Canada: University of Manitoba Press, 1972.

Cooper, William. "Reflections on Some Aspects of the Experimental Novel." *International Literary Annual,* 2 (1959), 29-36.

Cruickshank, John, ed. *French Literature and Its Background: The Twentieth Century* (#6). London: Oxford University Press, 1970.

—————. "Some Aspects of French Fiction, 1935-1960." *The Novelist as Philosopher.* Ed. John Cruickshank. London: Oxford University Press, 1962, 3-26.

Culler, Jonathan. *Structuralist Poetics: Structuralism, Linquistics and the Study of Literature.* London: Routledge and Kegan Paul, 1975.

Davis, Robert Gorham. "The Fantastic World of Anaïs Nin." *New York Times Book Review* (28 March 1948), 24.

Edel, Leon. *The Psychological Novel.* London: Rupert Hart-Davis, 1955.

Ellmann, Richard, and Charles Feidelson, eds. *The Modern Tradition.* New York: Oxford University Press, 1965.

Engler, Winifred. *The French Novel from Eighteen Hundred to the Present.* Trans. Alexander Gode. New York: Frederick Ungar, 1969.

Evans, Calvin. "Cinematography and Robbe-Grillet's *Jealosy.*" *Nine Essays in Modern Literature.* Ed. Donald E. Stanford. Baton Rouge, Louisiana: Louisiana State University Press, 1965, 117-128.

Evans, Oliver. *Anaïs Nin.* Carbondale, Illinois: Southern Illinois University Press, 1968.

—————. "Anaïs Nin and the Discovery of Inner Space." *Prairie Schooner,* 36 (1962), 217-231.

Farber, Marjorie. "Subjectivity in Modern Fiction." *Kenyon Review,* 7 (1945), 645-652.

102

Fisher, Ernst. *The Necessity of Art*. Trans. Anna Bastock. London: Penguin Books, 1963.

Fletcher, John. *New Directions in Literature*. London: Calder and Boyars, 1968.

Forster, E.M. *Aspects of the Novel*. London: Peguin Books, 1964.

Fort, Keith. "The Revolutionary New Novel." *Minnesota Review*, 7 (1967), 170-176.

Foucault, Michel. "Debut sur le roman." *Tel Quel*, 17 (1964), 12-54.

_____. *The Order of Things: An Archaeology of the Human Sciences* New York: Vintage Books, 1973.

Fowlie, Wallace. *Age of Surrealism*. Bloomington, Indiana: Indiana University Press, 1960.

_____. "The French Novel: Quests and Questions." *Contemporary European Novelists*. Ed. Siegfried Mandrel. Carbondale, Illinois: Southern Illinois University Press, 1968, 39-68.

Frank, Joseph. "Spacial Form in Modern Literature." *Sewanee Review*, 53 (1945), Part I, 221-240; Part II, 432-456; Part II, 643-653.

_____. *The Widening Gyre: Crisis and Mastery in Modern Literature*. New Brunswick, New Jersey: Rutgers University Press, 1963.

Friedman, Melvin J. "André Malraux and Anaïs Nin." *Contemporary Literature*, 2 (1970), 104-113.

Frohock, W. M. *Style and Temper: Studies in French Fiction 1925-1960*. Cambridge, Massachusetts: Harvard University Press, 1972.

Garzilli, Enrico. *Circles Without Center: Paths to the Discovery and Creation of Self in Modern Literature*. Cambridge, Massachusetts: Harvard University Press, 1972.

Gershman, Herbert. *The Surrealist Revolution in France*. Ann Arbor, Michigan: University of Michigan Press, 1969.

Gilman, Richard. "Total Revolution in the Novel." *Horizon*, 4 (1962), 96-101.

Glicksberg, Charles. "The Psychology of Surrealism." *Polemic*, 8 (1947), 46-55.

Goodheart, Eugene. *The Cult of the Ego: The Self in Modern Literature*. Chicago: University fo Chicago Press, 1968.

Grant, Damian. *Realism*. London: Methuen and Co., 1970.

Gras, Vernon, ed. *European Literary Theory and Practice from Existential Phenomenology to Structuralism*. New York: Delta, 1973.

Grossvogel, David. *Limits of the Novel: Evolutions of a Form from Chaucer to Robbe-Grillet*. New York: Oxford University Press, 1968.

Hagopian, John V. "Symbol and Metaphor in the Transformation of Reality into Art." *Comparative Literature*, 20 (1968), 45-54.

Harmes, Valerie, ed. *Celebration with Anaïs Nin*. Riverside, Connecticut: Magic Circle Press, 1973.

Harvey, W. J. *Character and the Novel*. Ithaca, New York: Cornell University Press, 1965.

Hassan, Ihab. *The Dismemberment of Orpheus*. New York: Oxford University Press, 1971.

_____. *Radical Innocence: Studies in the Contemporary American Novel*. Princeton, New Jersey: Princeton University Press, 1961.

Hocket, C. *The State of the Art*. The Hague: Mouton, 1967.

Holland, Norman. *The Dynamics of Literary Response*. New York: Oxford University Press, 1968.

Honan, Park, ed. "Realism, Reality, and the Novel." A Symposium in *Novel II, A Forum on Fiction*, 2 (1969), 197-211.

Howe, Irving, ed. *Literary Modernism*. New York: Fawcett World Library, 1967.

Jaeger, Patricia J. "Three Authors in Search of an Elusive Reality: Butor, Sarraute, Robbe—Grillet." *Critique: Studies in Modern Fiction*, 6 (1963), 65-85.

Kahler, Erich. *The Disintegration of Form in the Arts*. New York: George Braziller, 1968.

Kaminsky, Alice R. "On Literary Realism." *The Theory of the Novel: New Essays*. Ed. John Halperin. New York: Oxford University Press, 1974, 213-232.

Kermode, Frank. *The Sense of an Ending*. New York: Oxford University Press, 1967.

Kostelanetz, Richard, ed. *On Contemporary Literature*. New York: Avon Books, 1969.

Kreitler, Hans and Shulamith Kreitler. *Psychology of the Arts*. Durham, North Carolina: Duke University Press, 1972.

Kristiva, Julia. *Le Texte de roman: Approche sémiologigue d'une structure discursive transformationelle*. The Hague: Mouton, 1970.

LeSage, Larent. *The French New Novel*. University Park, Pennsylvania: Pennsylvania State University Press, 1962.

Lesser, Simon. *Fiction and the Unconscious*. New York: Vintage Books, 1957.

Levin, Harry. "What is Realism?" *Comparative Literature*, 3 (1951), 193-199.

_____. "Realism Reconsidered." *The Theory of the Novel: New Essays*. Ed. John Halperin. New York: Oxford University Press, 1974, 233-256.

Lewis, C. S. *An Experiment in Criticism*. London: Cambridge University Press, 1961.

Littlejohn, David. "The Anti-Realists." *Daedalus*, 92 (1963), 250-264.

Longman, Lester. "Criteria of Criticism in Contemporary Art." *Journal of Aesthetics*, 18 (1960), 285-293.

Loy, J. Robert. "*Things* in Recent French Literature." *PMLA*, 71 (1956), 27-41.

Luijpen, William A. *Phenomenology and Humanism*. Pittsburg, Pennsylvania: Duquesne University Press, 1966.

Lulacs, John. *The Passing of the Modern Age*. New York: Harper and Row, 1970.

MacNamera, Desmond. "Nin et Al." *New Statesman* (1 December 1967), 778-779.

Marcus, Steven. "The Novel Again." *Partisan Review*, 29 (1962), 159-195.

Matthews, J. H. *Surrealism and the Novel*. Ann Arbor, Michigan: University of Michigan Press, 1966.

Mercier, Vivian. *The New Novel from Queneau to Pinget*. New York: Farrar, Strause and Giroux, 1971.

McDowall, Arthur. *Realism: A Study in Art and Thought*. London: Constable and Co., 1918.

McEvilly, Wayne. "Two Faces of Death in Anaïs Nin's *Seduction of the Minotaur*." *New Mexico Quarterly*, 9 (1969), 179-192.

Miller, Henry. *The Cosmological Eye*. Norfolk, Connecticut: New Directions, 1939.

_____. *Letters to Anaïs Nin*. Ed. Gunther Stuhlmann. New York: G. P. Putman's Sons, 1965.

_____. "Un Être Etoilique." *The Henry Miller Reader*, Ed. Lawrence Durrell. New York: New Directions, 1959, 287-306.

Morris, Lloyd. "Anaïs Nin's Special Art." *New York Herald Tribune Book Review* (12 March 1950), 17.

Morrissette, Bruce. *Alain Robbe-Grillet.* New York: Columbia University Press, 1965.

_____. "International Aspects of the Nouveau Roman." *Contemporary Literature,* 11 (1970), 155-168.

_____. "The New Novel in France." *Chicago Review,.* 15 (1962), 1-19.

_____. *Les Romans de Robbe-Grillet.* Paris: Les Éditions de Minuit, 1963.

_____. "Theory and Practice in the Works of Robbe-Grillet." *Modern Language Notes,* 77 (1962), 257-267.

Morse, J. Mitchell. "The Choreography of 'The New Novel.'" *Hudson Review,* 16 (1963), 64.

Muir, Edwin. *The Present Age.* London: The Cresset Press, 1939.

Murray, Jack. "Mind and Reality in Robbe-Grillet and Proust." *Wisconsin Studies in Contemporary Literature,* 8 (1967), 407-420.

Nadeau, Maurice. *The French Novel Since the War.* London: Methuen and Co., 1967.

_____. *The History of Surrealism.* New York: Macmillan, 1965.

O'Brien, Justin. *The French Literary Horizon.* New Brunswick, New Jersey: Rutgers University Press, 1967.

Ortega y Gassett, José. *The Dehumanization of Art and Other Writings on Art and Culture.* Princeton, New Jersey: Princeton University Press, 1948.

_____. "The Doctrine of the Point of View." *The Modern Tradition.* Eds. Richard Ellmann and Charles Feidelson. New York: Oxford University Press, 1965, 91-92.

Oxenhandler, Neal. "Toward the New Aesthetic." *Contemporary Literature,* 2 (1970), 169-191.

Pettit, Philip. *On the Idea of Phenomenology.* Dublin: Scepter Books, 1969.

Peyre, Henri. *French Novelists of Today.* New York: Oxford University Press, 1967.

Phelps, Robert, ed. *Twentieth-Century Culture: The Breaking Up.* New York: George Braziller, 1965.

Phillips, William, ed. *Art and Psychoanalysis.* New York: Criterion Books, 1957.

Porter, Dennis. "Sartre, Robbe-Grillet, and the Psychotic Hero." *Modern Fiction Studies,* 16 (1970), 13-25.

Rahv, Philip. *Image and Idea*. Norfolk, Connecticut: New Directions, 1957.

Ricardou, Jean. *Pour une théorie du nouveau roman*. Paris: Éditions de Seuil, 1967.

_____. *Problemes du nouveau roman*. Paris: E'ditions de Seuil, 1967.

Rolo, Charles. "The Very Special World of Anaïs Nin." *Atlantic* (February 1950), 86.

Rosenfeld, Issac. "Psychoanalysis as Literature." *New Republic* (17 December 1945), 844-845.

Roudiez, Leon. *French Fiction Today: A New Direction*. New Brunswick, New Jersey: Rutgers University Press, 1972.

Rycroft, Charles. "Freud and the Imagination." *New York Review of Books*, 2 (1975), 26-30.

Seltzer, Alvin J. *Chaos in the Novel: The Novel in Chaos*. New York: Schocken Books, 1974.

Schneider, Duane. "The Art of Anaïs Nin." *The Southern Review*, 6 (1970), 506-514.

_____. *An Interview with Anaïs Nin*. Athens Ohio: Duane Schneider Press, 1970.

Scholes, Robert. *The Fabulators*. New York: Oxford University Press, 1967.

Scholes, Robert, and Robert Kellog. *The Nature of Narrative*. New York: Oxford University Press, 1966.

Scott, Nathan A., Jr. *Negative Capability: Studies in the New Literature and the Religious Situation*. New Haven, Connecticut: Yale University Press, 1969.

Sollers, Philippe. *Logiques*. Paris: Éditions de Seuil, 1968.

Spencer, Sharon. *Space, Time and Structure in the Modern Novel*. New York: New York University Press, 1971.

Spender, Stephen. *The Struggle of the Modern*. London: Hamish Hamilton, 1963.

Stevick, Philip, ed. *The Theory of the Novel*. New York: The Free Press, 1967.

Stoltzfus, Ben F. *Alain Robbe-Grillet and the New French Novel*. Carbondale, Illinois: Southern Illinois University Press, 1964.

Sypher, Wylie. *Loss of the Self in Modern Literature and Art*. New York: Vintage Books, 1964.

Thevenaz, Pierre. *What is Phenomenology and Other Essays*. Chicago: Quadrangle Books, 1964.

Under the Sign of Pisces: Anaïs Nin and Her Circle. (The Nin Newsletter). Eds. Richard Centing and Benjamin Franklin, V.

Walsh, D. "The Cognitive Content of Art." *Contemporary Studies in Aesthetics*. Ed. F. J. Coleman. New York: McGraw-Hill, 1968, 282-197.

Weightman, John. "Alain Robbe-Grillet." *The Novelist as Philosopher*. Ed. John Cruickshank. London: Oxford University Press, 1962, 230-252.

Weinstein, Arnold L. *Vision and Response in Modern Fiction*. Ithaca, New York: Cornell University Press, 1974.

White, John J. *Mythology in the Modern Novel: A Study of Prefigurative Techniques*. Princeton, New Jersey: Princeton University Press, 1971.

Wylie, Harold A. "Alain Robbe-Grillet: A Scientific Humanist." *Bucknell Review*, 15 (1967), 1-9.

Wylie, Harold A. "The Reality-Game of Robbe-Grillet." *French Review*, 40 (1967), 774-780.

Zinnes, Harriet. "Anaïs Nin's Work Reissued." *Books Abroad*, 37 (1963), 283-286.

ABOUT THE AUTHOR

Patricia A. Deduck

Patricia A. Deduck is Assistant Professor of English at Southwest Texas State University. She is a graduate of the State University of New York, College at Plattsburgh, where she received her B.A. degree, and holds an M.A. and Ph.D. in Comparative Literature from Indiana University.